Systems Management for UNIX

and UNIX-like Systems

N.G.Backhurst MIDPM
P.J.Davies, D.Phil.

SIGMA
PRESS

First published in 1986 by

Sigma Press
98a Water Lane, Wilmslow, SK9 5BB, England.

Printed in Malta by Interprint Limited
Reprinted 1988

British Library Cataloguing in Publication Data

Backhurst, N.G.
  Systems management under UNIX and UNIX-like
  systems.
  1. UNIX (Computer operating system)
  I. Title   II. Davies, P.J.
  005.4'3   QA76.76.063

ISBN 1-85058-049-9

Distributed by
John Wiley & Sons Ltd., Baffins Lane, Chichester, West Sussex, England.

For *Ruth*

For *May*

Warning

There are many types of Unix systems and even more Unix-like systems. In general these tend to be fairly similar but they are not identical.

It is quite common to find commands on one system which are not available on other systems. Alternatively you may find that the same command can do two very different jobs, like the **enable** command.

You should therefore not presume that a command on your system will be exactly like it is in this book, or for that matter any other general book. Before using any command, check with your own system documentation. Find out what the syntax used on your system is and what the effect of the command on your system will be.

If in doubt, contact your system supplier. With a bit of luck he or she might know the answer.

Preface

This book is for people who have a reasonable knowledge of computing and some knowledge of Unix or Unix-like systems, and who are responsible for the management or administration of a multi-user micro computer network running under Unix or a Unix-like operating system. The majority of concepts, however, are equally applicable to all types of micro computer installations. This is especially true in the areas of staffing, security and staff training.

Our aim has been to present the reader with the essential information in a non-technical manner to enable him or her to manage a Unix or Unix-like system. In addition, the underlying concepts behind the procedures are explained on the principle that the system manager should know what to do and also why the procedures are being carried out.

During the last four or five years, the terms, *system administration* and *system management*, have undergone a change in meaning. One factor behind this change has been the advent of powerful micro computers which has changed the traditional patterns of responsibility and staffing within computer departments.

This book has been written to give an insight into the activities which now come under the heading of system management.

There is no attempt in this book to delve into the technicalities of the command structures in Unix. Eric Foxley's book, **Unix for Superusers**, treats this subject in a comprehensive and straightforward manner. There is, similarly, no attempt to introduce Unix to a naive user, for which **Unixthe Book** by Banahan and Rutter is a good starting point.

CONTENTS

Chapter One

Introduction.

The history and development of Unix, in all its forms, has created a very powerful operating system for multi-user, multi- tasking mini computer and micro computer systems. This same development process, however, has not necessarily created an ideal operating system for commercial environments.

Taking this view of Unix and Unix-like operating systems, we have described what we think are the main areas of concern for the system manager. We do not imagine that you will want to read this book from cover to cover. Our aim, however, has been to make it possible to do so as painlessly as possible, while, at the same time, providing the essential reference material that you need to be able to find as everyday tasks demand.

Unix is so large and powerful it can be a real problem. It can also be fascinating, surprising and fun. As we wrote this book, both attitudes surfaced - sometimes at the the same time!

We hope that we have conveyed some of this in what we have written and that you will find as much pleasure in using Unix as we have had - and that, similarly, we have smoothed over the majority of the problems.

Background and History.

The trademark Unix is owned by Bell Laboratories, a division of the giant AT&T company. It is the name given to a family of related operating systems developed by Bell Laboratories.

In the late 1960s Bell Labs were involved in work on an interactive multi-user operating system called Multics. Sometime in 1968 it became increasingly clear to the Computing Science Research Department of Bell Labs that there were problems with the system. This led to a slow, but inevitable, withdrawal of Bell Labs from the Multics project during 1968 and 1969.

For staff at Bell Labs, like D. Ritchie, K. Thompson, J. Ossanna and M. McIlroy, who had been deeply involved in the Multics project, this withdrawal caused problems. During 1969 these people effectively started to search for an alternative to Multics. This involved looking at medium sized machines which they could use and lobbying to get Bell Labs to purchase such a machine. In addition, they began session working with blackboards and notes, developing ideas about how an operating system should work to give them the environment they needed.

Thompsom, Canaday and Ritchie outlined a file structure for such an operating system. This was to become the familiar Unix file structure. Thompson actually implemented a model of this file structure under Multics.

It was a process which was to give the final spur to the development of Unix.

In parallel, during 1969 Thompson had developed a simulation of the movement of the major bodies in the solar system. In it, a player would try to guide his spaceship, landing on planets and observing the landscape. This game, 'Space Travel', had first been written under Multics, then been translated into Fortran to run on a General Electric 635 under the GECOS operating system. Unfortunately this was not very satisfactory. The game was hard to control due to the way in which commands had to be entered. Worse still it was very expensive to play, because of the high cost of processing time on the big computer.

Thompson found in Bell Labs an old and little-used PDP-7 which had a first class display. With assistance from Ritchie he re- wrote the game to run on it. This served as a good foundation for preparing programs for this machine. Soon after, Thompson started to implement the proposed file system on the PDP-7, to which he added the basic structure that was required for an operating system.

This was soon followed by a small set of user-level utilities, which provided the means to copy or print files, simple file handling routines and a simple command interpreter. Very soon an Assembler was also added.

Up to this point, all the development had taken place on the General Electric system under GECOS with the programs being cross assembled and transferred to the PDP-7 on paper tape. Once the Assembler was installed on the PDP-7, the system became self standing.

By 1970, when Brian Kernighan suggested calling the system Unix, the operating system had basically the structure we know today. In 1970 the department also got a PDP-11 and the first transfer, or *port*, of Unix was made, though this did involve completely re- writing the kernel code for the new machine in Assembler, although it was actually written on the old PDP-7.

Kernighan and Ritchie had already developed the C language. Unix was now re-written, mostly in C. This offered a high degree of portability between systems as from now on it was only necessary to write the lowest level of hardware interface in Assembler, because the rest of the code could be in C and easily transferred from one system to another.

Up till the mid 1970's Unix was very much an internal matter for Bell Labs, but from mid 1970 onwards it began to be used in the academic world of colleges and universities. This process was very much helped during the year that Ken Thompson spent as a visiting professor at the University of California at Berkeley where he introduced Unix to the computer science department.

After he left Berkeley the professors and students there continued to develop Unix and write enhancements to it. Versions of this Unix were made available to a large number of universities and also adopted by a number of commercial system suppliers.

At the same time, Bell Labs actively encouraged the adoption of Unix in universities, both in the United States and in Europe. It was enthusiastically accepted by universities on both sides of the Atlantic.

Many people outside the academic world have taken this acceptance of Unix by the universities as a sign of its quality. This is not how it should be seen. A number of other operating systems were available at the time which were as good, if not better, than Unix. There were, however, powerful factors, not particularly intrinsic to Unix, which were influential in the adoption of Unix.

First, although Unix was not absolutely given away, it was supplied for a nominal price only. Compared with what was being asked for other operating systems, it was effectively free. Secondly, and far more importantly, the sites which adopted Unix obtained a copy of the source code and could alter it as they required. From the point of view of computer science departments in universities this was the most significant factor, as Unix was an operating system which they could play with and develop as they wanted.

A final and very important point was Unix's increasing portability. The universities often had quite a range of incompatible machines, as different manufacturers or benefactors donated systems. Although each machine may have been supplied with its own operating system, the ability to put Unix onto them all meant that department could run everything under the same operating system. This could result in far better use being made of the limited resources at the disposal of the universities.

As a result of this adoption of Unix by the academic world in the late 1970s, it has now become the main operating system upon which computer graduates are trained. In fact, many students at university during the late 1970s may never have had experience of any other operating environment.

This situation has now altered, however, because of the advent of low cost personal computers, and newer graduates will have experience of two or three operating systems, other than Unix.

It should be noted throughout this history and development process, no mention has been made about any commercial development of Unix. This is simply because Unix was never designed to be used in a commercial environment, since it was written to provide a program development environment. This is the use to which it was put in Bell Labs, and this was its original use in the universities.

In the early 1980s, two events took place which combined to create a new situation. First the price of computer power dropped radically - if not quite overnight, certainly within months. Secondly, the first wave of computer graduates trained on Unix started to obtain reasonably senior appointments with businesses and companies. This generation of graduates was given charge of adding computer systems to companies, and naturally favoured the operating system they knew, Unix.

This was what really brought Unix into the commercial application market. As it was the operating system which senior data processing staff knew how to use, many of the first decisions to introduce Unix into commercial environments were based not so much on the quality of Unix, but on the fact that senior computing staff found Unix the easiest system to use.

Once Unix started to penetrate the commercial marketplace, it became inevitable that application software would be developed for it. More importantly, newer versions of Unix began to take the requirements of the commercial user into account.

At the same time, the giant AT&T corporation was split up by the American government. No longer bound by the restrictions which had constrained the activities of Bell Labs, Unix began to be promoted actively in the commercial market. The result is that Unix is now probably the leading commercial multi-user, multi- tasking operating system on the market and most computer manufacturers and suppliers are offering systems which use it.

We are, however, also seeing a number of questions being raised over the advisability of using Unix in commercial application environments. This is partly because there is a new generation of computer staff who have come to computing from backgrounds other than the academic, which means that they have not necessarily had any of the experience in Unix that computer graduates have had. These people, often with a background in business administration, are at an equal disadvantage whatever system they select. They have therefore no prejudices or feelings in favour of Unix. They also tend to be more demanding with respect to system performance than the computer graduate, who is prepared to make allowances for the system, having a better understanding of the problems involved.

Secondly, different options are becoming available. One that has been increasingly adopted in many commercial applications is a single user personal computer, linked into a network with a common file server system for shared files. Single-user, micro- computers have become generally accepted in the office and executives have become used to their fast response time, and there is considerable opposition to the introduction of multi- user systems with their associated drop in response and performance.

A further aspect is the growing awareness that any multi-user, multi-tasking operating system supplied for general use is always a compromise. Many commercial situations have only one application running on the system. In such a case many of the facilities offered by systems like Unix are wasted. A dedicated operating system can and does supply a much better environment with fewer problems all round.

This is probably best summed up in the comment made by James Russell, a Scottish computer and data communications consultant: "The obvious answer is to make full use of Unix to develop your application software. It is hard to think of a better development environment. When your software is developed, run it under an operating enviroment, naturally also developed under Unix, but which has been specifically designed and developed for that application."

Though this comment was made particularly about large scale dedicated applications, many people in the computer industry now regard such views as applicable right across the range of mini and micro computer installations.

These views, however, do not suggest that the end of Unix is in sight, although they do mean that the System Manager must look at the selection of Unix as the prime operating system more critically. The presence, however, of a large number of systems already installed and running, the large quantities of associated software, and the commitment of major manufacturers and suppliers to Unix, in various forms, ensure that Unix is not finished. It is likely however that the role of Unix will change and that Unix will also have an increasingly important role in meeting specialised and particular demands.

There are already signs that the future of Unix will not be in supplying an overall operating system for a computer installation, but in supplying the core operating system used by the file server in a network. On that network a number of other computers will be operating under different operating systems.

If this is what is required, Unix will be able to supply it, for it has a high degree of flexibility and a great potential. We do, however, doubt if it will ever become the industry standard it was hailed as providing a few years ago. There is one basic problem here that cannot be avoided: Unix itself has not been standardised. Programs developed on one Unix system are not that easily ported to another despite any claims to the contary.

An anonymous quotation found scrawled in the margin of an article on Unix perhaps sums it all up: "We were promised a pearl, but it turned out to be cultured and there are signs it might be artificial."

Chapter Two

System Management under Unix.

System management is a relatively new phrase, and it should be carefully distinguished from the old mainframe term, *systems management*. Whereas that term was concerned with the planning and use of computer mainframe systems, system management is directed towards keeping a computer system functioning properly and effectively.

A second form of confusion can arise because of the way that Unix has developed. According to the usual Unix definition, derived mainly from the academic world in which Unix first became popular, the role of the system manager is confused with that of the system administrator. As Unix has moved from the self-contained world of academic computer departments into the mainstream of commercial computing, the terminology has not really kept pace.

Despite this, we think it important to insist on the newer term. In commercial systems, as we will see, the administrator has become a manager. In the process much of the specialist knowledge previously required of an administrator has become redundant, and new responsibilities and functions have been given to the system manager.

Within the academic environment, a Unix system administrator was an expert whose main function was keeping the system going. It was not unusual for the people filling this role to be referred to as GOD - the Guru On Duty. They were required to deal with systems which came complete with the original source code, but very little in the way of support and back up. In this extremely difficult situation, their task was very testing, and their knowledge of the intricacies of their system was likely to be extensive and profound. Since a major element in their academic work was likely to be concerned with the development and understanding of computing systems' potential this was obviously a very practical approach.

In contrast, the modern system manager, while still required to administer the computer system, faces a different range of problems, primarily centered on maintaining a computer in a commercial office. He or she will have no access to source code, nor need it. It is highly unlikely that a system manager will have much formal training, and he or she may well be a relatively naive user. In such circumstances, there is little direct comparison with the role of the academic system administrator, and this explains the need for the new job description, system manager. Thus, although attitudes may still not have changed throughout the Unix world, it is important to grasp this major change.

There are additional tasks faced by system managers, that did not fall within the range of work usually associated with a system administrator. For instance, the system manager will often be responsible for the recruitment, selection and training of staff and this can form a significant part of his or her work. The economic allocation of time and resources is also a fundamental requirement. Restraints that may well not have worried a system administrator may cause problems for the system manager. He or she will, for example, only have a strictly limited amount of time for carrying out his or her essential tasks of managing the machine, since every second that the machine is not functioning in its main commercial role is likely to be a direct drain on company profits.

There is still a difficulty, however, in that many senior people who have the job of designing or selling computer systems were trained or had their experience before 1980, and still tend to cling to the outmoded concepts. This may cause problems of understanding. However, this difference in role between the old academic system administrator and the new commercial system manager is being more widely recognised now, and for this reason the newer term is being used much more frequently to identify managerial and administrative functions within commercial offices.

In addition to this change in emphasis and approach, there is another change which can be no less significant. Computers used to be supported by a team of specialist staff: operators, data clerks, data managers, documentation clerks, database managers and a host of specialist programmers. Nowadays, these specialists are likely to have been replaced by non-specialist staff who use the computer as part of their ordinary work and who have the support of relatively few specialist support staff. Indeed, such support staff as do exist will probably only spend part of their time engaged in support, having other responsibilities possibly unrelated to the effective running of the computer system.

Previously specific tasks related to computer systems would be associated with particular categories of staff. The tendency now is for several of these functions to be combined into the responsibility of one employee so that, in a small office, one person may well undertake all the functions previously carried out by three or more people. The tasks themselves, however, have remained virtually unchanged and by examining the old staff structure and then seeing the changes that have been made, a better understanding of the complexity of the system manager's work can be gained.

The first area was that of the *computer operator*, whose basic task was to input data into the system, and deal with the information that forms the system's output. The operator usually worked on the computer using a terminal, made up of a keyboard and a visual display unit. The operator, in general, was hardly concerned with the workings of the computer and mainly dealt with one or two specific application, such as a word processing program or an accounting program.

Above the computer operator was a supervisor whose task was to manage a group of operators. It was his or her responsibility to assign work to the operators and to supervise them while they were carrying out their tasks. The supervisor was generally responsible for a group of operators who were engaged on a common task, rather than, say, a number of people who happened to use the same machine for different purposes. In that way, the person who had responsibility for word processing might have had six operators working for him or her, of whom four were working on one system, while two were working on a different one, but all would be engaged in, say, word processing. Incidentally, there were real advantages in such an arrangement since even if a machine did stop functioning, it meant that a particular task could still carry on within a company or organisation.

System administrator

Computer operator supervisors also undertook some or all of the tasks allocated to system supervisors, who were responsible for a range of jobs associated with one computer system. For instance, they ensured that the system was powered up properly, that the operating system and all the various supporting programs which have to be resident in the system to support the required application programs were present and working effectively, and that all peripheral devices, such as printers and tape and disk drives, were working correctly and had the right materials.

System supervisors were also responsible for identifying and acting upon any error messages they received from their terminal, monitoring and logging the computer's performance, particularly whenever unusual or unexpected events had taken place, taking note of the quality of all printed documents, and acting to correct any errors if they occurred.

In addition such mundane tasks as cleaning all equipment that is sensitive to dust and preserving good and comprehensive backups of all files, fell to the system supervisor.

Each system, then, required its supervisor, in order to maintain its day to day running.

Then there was the *system administrator* who had a similar role to that of a system supervisor but who was responsible for more than one computer.

The role of the *data processing administrator* was to co- ordinate and maintain all the general data processing activities within one network, which consists of two or more computers linked so that they can interchange data. His or her prime responsibility was to allocate the network's resources between the various tasks that are carried out within the network.

The *network administrator* was responsible for the efficient operation of the telecommunications network, including the establishment of physical connections, monitoring the network's operation, making necessary corrections, and liaising with remote sites.

The *network manager* had the overall responsibility for the networking system and was required to maintain the network, both its software and its various hardware elements. These duties were usually combined with those of the data processing manager, who had overall responsibility for the running of the complete computer department.

Above the system manager, the *data processing manager* was responsible to top management for the introduction of information systems, understanding and meeting the data processing requirements of the organisation, and planning how to cope with present and future needs. The demands placed upon the system by the data processing manager were met by the system administrator allocating appropriate resources. In addition, the effective running of the system, including corrections and maintenance of the file system, for example, were the job of the system administrator.

A further responsibility of the system administrator was to design a proper support structure within which the system supervisor and the network manager could work.

These job and task classifications would have been recognised within any computer installation which was larger than a single- user, stand-alone system.

The vestiges still remain. If this is not immediately apparent, it will become so, by adjusting some of these separate functions or combining them. Most modern installations have a system manager, who combines the role of data processing manager, supervisor and operator. On the other hand, the job of network manager and system administrator no longer exist within computer systems that were designed after about 1980 for commercial use.

Nowadays, instead of a data processing manager, a system administrator, operator supervisor and network manager, there is likely to be only a system manager who will combine all these roles. Anyone who then has a need to use the system, will use it as and when necessary for whatever function is required at any one moment and the system manager will make all the necessary adjustments.

In such a situation, the system manager faces a whole range of problems, which can effectively be reduced to one: maintaining a computer system which efficiently meets the needs of his or her firm or organisation. Under this all-embracing heading will fall: routine operations to keep the machine running, or to allow recovery after a machine failure; maintaining the file system and taking backups; allocating the resources in the system in the most cost-effective way so that users have appropriate access to the machine and also maintaining the hardware and software so that it does not fail at crucial moments. This latter aspect will include ensuring that the system is secure from unauthorised access, controlling the access that users have to the machine and ensuring that the data held on the computer system is preserved in its proper form. In addition, the system manager often has a staff function, which means being responsible for the recruitment, selection and training of the staff who will be using the computer system.

A final responsibility of the system manager is to take a very cynical view of the capabilities of computer equipment, which means being prepared at all times for a catastrophe, such as a complete system crash, and having appropriate procedures which will allow the most effective recovery, the quickest analysis of the reasons for the crash and immediate counter-measures to prevent a reoccurrence.

Chapter Three
The Operational Environment.

3.1 Environmental Considerations.

In general, modern mini computers and micro computers are designed to tolerate a wide range of environmental conditions, but temperature and humidity can affect them adversely. It is sensible, therefore, to provide a reasonable environment which avoids extremes. Fewer problems can then be expected.

As a system manager, you should acknowledge the importance of the environment within which you expect the computer to work. You have first to ensure that proper power supplies, adequate anti- static precautions and, for example, air-conditioning, are available before the computer is installed. Secondly you have to ensure that the environment remains stable.

3.2 Power Supplies.

Modern mini and micro computers tend not to be as sensitive to power supply problems as earlier computers, but they are still relatively sensitive to fluctuations in power.

The exact quality of this sensitivity varies throughout the world. Most modern power supply units in mini and micro computers can generally cope with a 10 per cent variation in voltage, and sometimes a 15 per cent variation. In Europe this allows a drop of some 22 volts, while in the USA, because the power supply is usually 110 volts, the figure is approximately only 11 volts. A 12 volt drop in power in the States can therefore have serious effects, while the same 12 volt drop is well within the tolerance of the equipment in Europe.

There are three main types of faults in power supplies of which the system manager needs to be aware: noise, fluctuations in voltage and disruptions to the power supply.

Noise can be caused by the generating authority itself, by the distribution system and some by local factors. Even the switching on and off of an electrical appliance in an office can cause such noise, as can lighting. Lighting can, indeed, cause noise not only in the mains supply but also in the connections between the computer and its peripherals, such as printers and modems.

Noise can be dealt with by fitting line filters, not only between the computer and the power supply, but also between the computer and peripherals wherever there is a long cable between them.

The voltage of the electrical power supply is generally considered to be stable, but, in fact, surges in power are really quite common. They are of two types: spikes and sags, which last a short time, and surges and brownouts, which last much longer.

As suggested earlier, modern power supply units can cope with moderate surges and brownouts. It is a sensible precaution, however, to check the capabilities of your computer's power supply and also the reliability of the local power supply. If there are any doubts at all, it is essential to install a voltage regulator, in order to even out such variations.

Total disruption of the power supply, whether for an instant or for a longer period, is potentially very dangerous. The new generation super micro computers are being provided with protection against such disruption. But the protection systems have two deficiencies. Usually they are designed to prevent damage to the file system rather than protect the data in the system at the time of the disruption. Secondly, they do not allow the computer to carry on processing, which can often be essential.

The answer is to install an uninterruptible power supply of one kind or another. In broad terms, these can divided into those that allow you to maintain the system in full running condition for a prolonged period of time and those designed to support the system long enough to achieve an orderly shutdown. The type that you select will be related to the demands on your particular system.

The one common element, however, in whichever uninterruptible power supply you choose is that there should be a proper warning signal to inform you that the power supply has gone down. It might seem that such an interruption in the power supply would be obvious, but the disruption might be solely to the socket into which the computer is plugged. Since it can be a sensible precaution to have a separate power supply for the computer, to isolate it from noise, for example, this is not an unlikely situation. If the circuit breaker for the computer's circuit is tripped, it might be possible to overlook it, especially if the computer appears to be continuing to work. Only when the uninterruptible power supply is exhausted would the problem be apparent, with serious results.

It is important to ensure, too, that you fit an uninterruptible power supply and not merely a back up power supply. With a back up power supply there can be a short, but destructive, gap between power failure and the back up power supply switching in. In other applications this may well be acceptable, but it is quite disastrous for a computer system. An uninterruptible power supply is specifically designed to ensure that there is no such gap.

In places where there is an unreliable power supply, there may well already be back up power supplies and it may not be appreciated that this is not sufficient. It is necessary to insist on the dangers and the need to ensure a proper uninterruptible power supply, even to a reluctant management.

Nevertheless it is certain that there will be problems at some stage during the operation of computer equipment. The effects of such problems can be varied:

- Loss or corruption of data files.

- Errors in program operation.

- A program crash.

- Faulty data transfer between networked systems, or to and from peripherals.

- Physical damage to the computer and its peripherals.

Loss of data files is not a major problem if the system is properly administered. It should be possible to restore the data from the routine back up files, without too much effort.

A more serious possibility is the corruption of data files, which can be undetected and carried forward into updated files. Major errors can develop in such circumstances.

The following case illustrates this point. A file which contained the interest rate levels used by a small finance house became corrupted. As a result, interest was paid at 0.2% rather than 0.01%. Interest paid out in a 31 day month amounted to £63.895, rather than £3.3036 per thousand pounds. Such a significant difference clearly would not go unnoticed, but if the figure had been changed to 0.012%, it may well have. Although the difference in payments would have been small, cumulatively the effect would have been serious.

Errors in the operation of programs can also result in incorrect data being written into files, with similar results.

On the other hand, a complete program crash would probably not be so much of a problem. Usually, such an event is immediately obvious, and the program can be rerun, if the original data is still extant.

Faulty transfer of data can again result in corrupted data files, which are the bane of the system manager's life.

Yet the most catastrophic event is a complete power failure that occurs while a disk is being written to. This can result in a complete disk drive head crash, which can irreparably damage the disk. In that case not only is the data lost, but the hardware needs to be replaced as well.

3.3 Temperature Control.

Most modern mini and micro computer systems can work effectively within a temperature range of 5 to 45 degrees, Centigrade. Yet experience will show that at the extremes problems can occur, particularly with higher temperatures. One reason is that a hot spot can build up within a computer, especially around the power supply and certain other components. This can raise the temperature quite respectably above the ambient temperature with awkward results. In addition, it is quite possible for a few days of very hot, or very cold, weather to occur, which will cause problems.

The addition of fans, humidifiers or even adequate ventilation can usually make the difference between safety and danger.

A safe operational temperature for computer systems is probably between 15 and 30 degrees Centigrade. If the temperature where the computer is installed is regularly outside this range, you should consider fitting proper air-conditioning in order to protect your valuable equipment and data.

Besides the precautions outlined above, the system manager ought to be aware of changes that can affect the environment within which the computer works. In winter, for example, your staff may well want additional heating, which can affect the temperature around the computer. Such changes can soon have an effect as can, say, the failure of the heating system itself. In such a case, if the temperature is approaching the operational minimum, it is essential to close the system down properly. It is far better to close the system down while it is still running, rather than wait until your data is corrupted.

It should be borne in mind that it is often small environmental changes which can cause the most problems, with devastating results. Even the relocation of a dividing screen in an open plan office can radically alter the temperature around a computer system. If the computer becomes exposed to full sunlight, for example, hot spots can develop within the computer's casing, with consequential increases in the internal temperature.

In short, you will need to be alert to the changes that occur in any office. And as a general rule of thumb, ensure that the computer is not in direct sunlight at any time.

3.4 Cables.

It is usually assumed that once a system has been properly installed, with all cables securely attached, it will remain like that. In practice, cables can and do become loose, with inevitably awkward results.

It is a sensible practice to make routine checks of all cables and their connections. How often this is necessary will depend on the particular installation but, obviously, the more the equipment is moved and the more the system is used, the more likelihood there is of problems with cables and their connections.

In addition, every time you start up the system, have a quick look at the cables and their connections, just to make sure that nothing is out of place. Such an elementary precaution can save a great deal of frustration later!

3.5 Disk and Tape Head Cleaning.

Deposits of oxide build up on both flexible disk and streamer tape heads when they are used. These deposits impair the performance of the equipment, and can result in errors in both reading and writing data.

It is good practice to clean the heads regularly, using special cleaning disks and tapes. These can be obtained from your computer system supplier or good computer stores.

Such cleaning is essential if you want to ensure that your system is reliable, and it should be carried out on a regular and routine basis. On a heavily-used system, such cleaning should be carried out weekly, while a more lightly used system should probably have the heads cleaned once a month.

3.6 System Log Books.

This section is entitled System Log Books, not System Logs, and this distinction is important.
It has generally been regarded as good practice to keep a record of what is taking place in a computer system. In the old days of batch processing this was done by writing a log entry into a book each time a new batch was put onto the system.

With real time interactive computing systems, there has been a development of automatic logging of certain activities by the operating system. As Unix provides a wide variety of methods to do this, there has been an increasing tendency for users to rely totally on the logs kept by the operating system. This has two weaknesses.

First there is no way that the operating system can have knowledge of, and thereby log, activities which do not affect the operating system itself. Even when an operating system does have some knowledge of an activity, such knowledge is very often necessarily incomplete. For instance, the system may be able to keep a record of when the disk format command was used. It cannot know that the disk formatted came from a red pack or a blue pack, if it was a new disk or you were re-formatting, or the code number printed on the disk. Such information is external to the computer system. It therefore has to be kept in a form external to the computer, namely in a log book.

The second weakness of computer maintained logs is when the system goes down. If a system failure results in the loss of files, this can mean that the log files are also lost. Since this can have serious repercussions, even where information is held in system logs, it is a sensible precaution to keep a written log book.

One point to note here is that the currrent increase in usage of VDU (visual display unit) terminals has increased the need for keeping a system log. Traditionally, the Unix system consol would be a teletype terminal. Indeed, many reference books on Unix state that the console should be a teletype terminal. This meant that a hard copy was produced of all commands entered at that terminal and of all messages received at that terminal. Whether this is desirable or not, with modern systems it is just not practical. Most commercial systems nowadays have mainly VDU terminals.

A system log book can provide you with a quick and easy check as to when procedures were carried out. This is particularly important with respect to cable checks, as discussed in the previous chapter. These may only be fully carried out at long intervals and it is difficult to judge the intervals without having a log of when they were last carried out.

The log itself need not be extremely detailed, and can comprise a few dated and timed notes. You will soon realise what you need to record, and how much detail you require.

An example of a system log is given below:

28-05-85 System started up at 08.00
          Fault developed on monitor on terminal 3. Monitor replaced 14.25

          Laser printer toner refilled 16.30

          System close down 18.45

29-05-85 System started up at 08.00
          Complete back up of file system taken 16.00

          Security copies taken to Wansworth office by messenger

          System close down 18.30

3.6.1 The Superuser's Log.

In many ways the superuser's log is the most important piece of documentation that you can keep. Before we consider the reasons for this, it is necessary to explain what it is.

Basically, any time you do anything on the computer as a superuser you should write down what you do and why you have done it, in a log. It is important that we stress the word write. If you keep the log in a book, not on the system, you will still have an effective record if the system goes down.

In this log you should also write down what the results are. Then, should something go wrong, you can look back and see what you have done and probably work out where you went wrong. More importantly quite often if you write down a comand before you carry it out, you think about the consequences of that command and may well decide to tackle the problem in another way.

18

Finally, and in our opinion most importantly, you will build up a textbook of techniques to use on your system. Every system is different and general books and manuals cannot do more than generalise. Sometime or other you will come across a problem which belongs strictly to your own system. You will have to find the solution. That problem may not come up again for some time, but if it does, you or your successor can look back in the log and find out what was done last time.

Even if you were not successful last time, it helps. At least you will know what not to do. In system management, like bomb disposal, we have learnt far more finding out what not to do than from finding out what to do.

3.6.2 Disk Log Book.

Another important special log book is the disk log book and, although here we use the term disk, we also include tape of course. In this book are kept records of all removable magnetic media used on the system.

Each disk or tape, as it is formatted, should be given a reference number, physically recorded on the disk or tape label. In the log book you should record:

- When it was formatted.

- From which batch it came.

- To whom it is allocated

If this procedure is followed a number of problems can be avoided. First, because all magnetic media wears out, it is advisable to stop using removable storage media which has been in use for any length of time. Secondly, as the history of each disk should be recorded, it can quickly be seen if a number of disks from a batch are found to be faulty. If this does happen the the whole batch must be regarded as suspect.

An entry from a disk log is given below:

23 May	10 5.25"	SSDD	Maxwell	Consort
10501	Sales			
10502	Sales			
10503	Sales			
10504	Admin		Damaged by misuse - scrapped	
10505	Admin			
10506				
10507				
10508			Formatting error - return to supplier	
10509				
10510				

In this record we are dealing with ten disks. The first line tells us they were formatted on May 23rd. They are five and a quarter inch single sided double density disks produced by Maxell. They have been supplied by Consort. Of the ten, five have been issued, three to sales and two to administration. Of those two, one had been damaged by misuse. As you can also see in the log, five disks have not been issued. One of these disks has had a formatting error and been returned to the supplier for a replacement. This level of detail is probably nearly all that is required in general.

As a minor point, it might have been useful if the form of misuse outlined in the log had been recorded. If the log showed that putting coffee cups on disks was common, then some user training might be indicated.

There is, perhaps, one further item which would have been useful to know, but is missing from this example: that is when the box came into stock. If it had been sitting about in the stock room for some months one might want to question how it was stored if a number of errors were found.

Not clear, but something that can be gleaned from this record is the batch the disks came from. In actual fact it is recorded, but if you don't know the system used it would be unclear. The first two numbers represent the batch number in the year, the last two which disk from the box, with the numbers in between representing the box itself. This might be clearer if the heading had been:

23 May	10 5.25" SSDD	Maxwell	Consort
Batch 10	Box 5		
01	Sales		
02	Sales		

The layout of written logs, naturally, must be up to you. Find the system which you can use, then use it, perhaps taking the example above as your starting point.

Chapter Four

Superuser and Privileged Users.

You will find, on any multi-user system, that there is a need for somebody who can undertake activities which are not available to the normal user. In Unix and Unix-like systems this need is fulfilled by the superuser.

A superuser can access all files on the system and undertake any task which is within the capabilities of Unix. All Unix protections and permissions are bypassed for the superuser. For this reason the superuser login should always be password protected.

In so far as the system is concerned any user who has the UID of zero and the GID of zero is a superuser. It is normal practice for the superuser to be known by the login name of **root** (see section on login names). On some systems this is even compulsory. Where it is not compulsory there is some merit in considering having a different login name for the superuser logon, though he or she may come up on the system as root (see section on logon).

4.1 Superuser Status: Dangers and Precautions.

The superuser is all powerful on the system. If you as a superuser give the system a command, provided the system knows the command, it will carry it out. This will be done no matter what the consequences of that action. Sometimes the consequences can be far from desirable.

It is therefore advisable for the superuser to take a few precautions:

-Unless there is no alternative, never work on the system as the superuser. Although many system administration functions require that you use restricted commands, these are often carried out by shell scripts called up by privileged users.

-If you are tired, fatigued or ill, do not take on superuser status.

-Be very careful when using any command which might result in irreparable damage to the system.

-Where a command has an interactive option, such as **rm**, use it. If you make a mistake at least you get a second chance.

-Whenever you find that you are using the same sequence of commands over and over again, write them into a shell script. Then you can call them up with just one command, so reducing the risk of typing errors.

-Where there is a choice of using a powerful command to carry out a task in a short while, or using a less powerful command which will take longer, opt for the latter. An illustration of a particularly dangerous procedure is the recommendation which is often made to use **rm -r** for removing the directories and files of a deleted user. Though this works most efficiently, it also removes any other user's files which are in those directories. It is far better to take the slower but more certain method of going through all the directories and removing the files with the usual **rm** command.

4.2 Privileged Users.

The superuser has the group identification of zero. Any other user who has this group identification will also be regarded by the system as being in the same group as the superuser, though they will not have the superuser's privileges.

Any user on the system can set the permissions on files which he or she owns for the different classes of users on the system.
The system recognises three settings:

-For the owner.

-For users of the same group.

-For all others.

The second setting is the useful one for setting up privileged users. It is therefore advisable to make as many tasks as possible performable by users in the system manager's group, that is users with the group id of zero, or users who can change to that group id. This can be done by setting the group users' permissions on the files.

Even where you have a command which you cannot make directly available to non-superusers, access can be provided through shell scripts with the **SUID** bit sets.

The **SUID** bit is an additional flag bit in the permission field which, if set, indicates to Unix that the process initiated by that file should take the effective user ID of the owner of the file and not of the user. The status of the **SUID** bit can be set with the **chmod** command. The normal syntax for doing this would be:

```
chmod u+s [filename]
```

You have to ascertain that the file has read and execute permissions for your group, before this would be effective. These can be given with **chmod** using:

```
chmod g+rx
```

An advantage of allowing privileged users to carry out certain administration tasks, especially on commercial systems, is that the system does not become over-reliant on one user being present. There are tales of horror told about sites where new staff joining the firm have been unable to access the computer system for nearly a month, because the system manager was on holiday and nobody else had write permission to the password file. Such a situation is certainly an argument for having a utility or shell script to add users to the system, and giving execute permission on that to members of a privileged users group.

As a final point: never log onto the system as superuser. Log on as a normal user and change to superuser by means of the **su** command when required.

There are two advantages to this. First it keeps you from getting into the habit of logging in as **root**. Once you start doing so you are likely to log in as the superuser for quite mundane tasks.

Secondly, the system maintains a log of all use of the **su** commands to take superuser status. Some systems go further and also log all the commands used, which can at times be useful.

One way to avoid direct logins as **root** is to amend the login program so that it will not accept logins for user names which are those of superusers. This option, however, is not normally available to users on commercial systems who do not have access to source code.

Chapter Five

Starting the System up and Closing Down.

The first task which faces the Unix system manager is how to get the system started. Unfortunately, with most Unix and Unix like systems it is not possible merely to switch them on. In addition, there is no universally adopted procedure for starting up a Unix system.

However, there is a set of procedures which have to be performed on any Unix system to get it up and running. These are the subject of this chapter, and are, in brief:

-The system has to be physically switched on.

-The kernel software has to be loaded into memory.

-The consistency of the file system has to be checked.

-The system has to be put into a multi-user mode.

5.1 Switching the System on.

There are no hard or fast rules concerning this. Every hardware manufacturer seems to have produced its own procedures for the actual task. In fact some manufacturers seem to have produced more than one. We know of at least one installation where there are two computer systems from the same manufacturer, both based on the same model of computer, but with totally different physical start up procedures.

There is a general rule which applies to all computer systems, whether or not they are Unix type systems: always switch on the power to peripheral devices, like printers, before switching on the main central processor unit (CPU). This avoids the possibility of damage occuring to the system due to power glitches produced by switching on the peripherals. The reverse, of course, applies when you are switching a system off, when you should always switch the CPU off first. Because this is only a general rule, a caveat applies: there are some hardware systems which require the CPU to be switched on before certain peripherals. Such requirements should be described in the manufacturer's documentation. In principle though, unless advised specifically to do otherwise, switch peripherals on before the CPU.

5.1.1 Key Switches.

One item which always comes up at this stage is the question of key switches. This is a matter which is more relevant to the security of the system, and it is discussed in more depth in that section, but a few words are appropriate here.

Most super-micros have some form of key switch which physically prevents unauthorised starting up of the system. These may be divided into two types: power switch key switches, and system control lock switches.

In the former type, where the key switch controls the power switch, the key has to be used to switch the power to the system on or off. This is useful for controlling unauthorised start up, but for little else. The system control lock switches, as their name suggests, actually lock the system controls. This means that to change the system controls, you have to unlock the system physically. This provides a far better form of security.

There are, in addition, a few systems which have both type of key switch.

5.1.2 Normal Booting Sequence.

The process of starting the system up is called Initial Program Load, normally abbreviated to IPL. This is more commonly known nowadays as *booting*.

The first stage of booting is undertaken by firmware, that is the computer system, and the latter stages by software loaded in from some form of secondary storage. Many systems presume that the loading will be undertaken from a specific device. On such systems the start up procedure usually consists of powering up, or resetting, after which the process is fairly automatic for the first stage.

There is one problem with systems that boot from a specific device, in that should the device be damaged, booting is prevented. This is generally avoided by allowing the system to be booted from any of the standard secondary storage devices on the system. Such an approach should be preferred when selecting a system. Where you have a choice of boot device, you are normally required to indicate on which device booting is to be carried out.

A further advantage of being able to boot from a selected device, at least for development systems, is that it can allow you to boot up under a non-standard version of the operating system.

Whether it is working on a default or a specified device, the first thing which happens is that the system reads from block 0 of the boot device. Block 0 is not part of the normal Unix file system and cannot under normal circumstances be written to. If you have to put the initial boot program onto block 0, you will have to use either the **dd** command or a special boot install shell script which is found on some systems.

From this stage onwards the procedure varies markedly, especially between commercial and development systems. The next two stages, however, are normally handled automatically by commercial systems which take default values held in the boot program.

The boot program will ask for the name of a supplementary or second stage boot program. The normal name for this program is /boot. This program will normally be held in the outermost file system on the boot device.

It is worth giving a word of warning at this point. Be careful when you type the name in. At this stage your console will have no correcting facilities. If you make a typing error you will have problems, which is a good argument for having the second stage name set as a default name in the first stage boot program.

Once the second stage Unix program has been loaded you will be prompted by the boot system prompt, normally a colon ':', to enter the name of the main Unix kernel. This stage is highly system dependent and you should consult your documentation for details.

When the Unix kernel has been loaded, it starts up automatically and carries out a test to establish the size of main memory. This is undertaken by accessing each memory address, working upwards until an error is encountered. After this the process init will be started automatically by the system.

init is stored in the directory /etc, so the full path name is /etc/init. This pathname is embedded in the Unix kernel. If it is necessary to use a different init program, that program has to be installed under /etc with the name init. Be careful about installing new init programs because if they fail, for any reason, the only way you can boot the system will be to boot from an alternative device.

Once the init program is running it will start up the single user shell, sometimes called the superuser shell. The system is now in a position where the system manager can carry out administrative activities prior to going into multi-user mode.

Exactly what administrative tasks are carried out will depend on the precise circumstances and nature of the system. One task however must be carried out, and this is the file system consistency check. (See the section on f s c k.)

There are a number of variations at this stage, all of which are designed to get around a fundamental security problem. If you have booted the system under the normal IPL procedure, you come up in single user mode as the superuser. This means that you have unlimited access to the system.

There are three main approaches to avoiding the problems, such as breaches of security, that this can cause. The first answer is for the system to come up in superuser mode, but ask for a password. If the incorrect password is entered the system can be closed down, or a re-boot carried out.

A second approach is to carry out f s c k automatically and then for the system to come up in multi-user mode. From the security point of view this can be a desirable method, especially when you have systems at sites where there is not a high level user normally in attendance. It does have the disadvantage, however, of not presenting you with that useful single user stage during boot, so that you can carry out system administration activities.

An answer to this consequence is a third approach. During boot up, the system can be made to pause for a set period. If during this period a signal is entered such as a specific key depression, then the system will come up in single user mode, otherwise it will come up as a multi-user system. The disadvantage of this is that unless it comes up in single user mode requesting a password, there is no security element here.

An important point to keep in mind here is that at this stage no secondary file systems have been mounted. This means that only those commands which are present in the r o o t file system are available for use.

5.2.1 date.

Many systems these days have a real time clock system which maintains the time and date. Where this is the case the date and time will normally be read in automatically by the IPL procedures. If however you are working on a system without a real time clock, or if for some reason the date given by the real time clock is not correct, you will have to enter the date and time, making use of the Unix d a t e command (some IPL's invoke this automatically for you).

The standard format for entering the date as given in the System V documentation is month, day, hour, minutes, year, all in numeric form. The syntax is:

```
date [ mmddhhmm[yy] ] [ +format ]
```

Entering **date 0817003086** would be to enter the date as 17th August 1986, with the time set at 30 minutes past midnight.

The format argument allows you to set the format in which the date will be printed. To use this you have to start the argument with a + and then list the field descriptors as required. These are given in the System V documentation as:-

n   insert a new-line character.

t   insert a tab character.

m   month of year - 01 to 12.

d   day of month - 01 to 31.

y   last two digits of year - 00 to 99.

D   date as mm/dd/yy.

H   hour - 00 to 23.

M   minute - 00 to 59.

S   second - 00 to 59.

j   day of year - 001 to 366.

w   day of week - Sunday = 0.

a   abbreviated weekday - Sun to Sat.

h   abbreviated month - Jan to Dec.

r   time in AM/PM notation.

Each field descriptor has to be preceded by a % sign in the format string. It will then be replaced in output by the corresponding value.

Therefore to set the format to print the time followed by the date written as days and months the command is:

```
= date '+TIME:%T%n%a:%d %h 19%y'
```

This will generate:

```
TIME 11:45:30
Thu: 9 Jan 1986
```

This can be very useful, but there is one problem. The date command seems to be the command which is most altered by system suppliers. Even with what are supposed to be standard Unix System V systems, it is no supprise to find that the date command has been amended to make it 'easier to use'. This generally seems to consist of fixing the format in the style they think it should be in and removing your ability to amend the format.

It should be noted that **date** can be used only by a superuser.

5.3 Going Multi User.

Once all the activities which the system manager needs to carry out by way of system maintenance in single user mode have been completed, the next stage is to go into multi-user mode. This is achieved by exiting from the single user shell, normally with **control-d**, though this can vary from system to system. In at least one case we are aware of, it requires switching the key switch from single user position to multi-user, for example.

The **init** process then sets up the system for multi-user mode. This is done in two stages: first the setting up of the general system, then the setting up of the various terminals connected to the system.

The procedures followed during these stages are highly system dependent and you should refer to your system documentation for details. The important thing to remember is that the procedures for the general setting up of the system are held in the file **/etc/rc**. Details of the terminals which are connected to the system are held in the file **/etc/ttys**.

Once these processes have been completed, the login message will be displayed. The system is now in the multi-user mode.

5.4 Closing the System down.

It might be argued that being able to close the system down is somewhat more important than being able to start the system up correctly. In an effort to keep the volume of disk traffic to a minimum Unix makes use of areas of memory to store data which is being read from or written to disk. This has the advantage that many accesses can be undertaken to the file without any physical access to the disk needing to take place. It has the disadvantage that should the system cease operation for any reason before this information has been written back to the file, the result will be a corrupted file system.

To close down a Unix system safely, two steps have to be taken. First all processes have to be killed. Secondly you must ensure that the disk system has been correctly updated.

There is, of course, a further proviso on this. The tasks outlined above must be carried out in a way which is acceptable to the users. In theory you could quite easily carry out the commands by entering a system **kill** command, then a **sync** command. Unfortunately if you did this you would have a number of protests from users who were on the system at the time and lost the work they were engaged in.

What is needed is some form of orderly procedure to close down the system which will allow users to finish what they are doing and get off the system. The generally accepted procedure is as follows:

- Issue an initial warning to all users that the system is going to be closed down in five minutes.

- Repeat the message at least once.

- Give final notice that the system is closing down.

- Kill all processes on the system.

- Issue the **sync** command.

- Switch off the system.

31

It is necessary to explain the procedure in more detail, of course. The first thing you must do is send a message to all users that the system is going to be closed down. This can be achieved by using the command **wall**. This stands for: write to all.

```
wall 'System closing down 5 minutes'
```

wall must be sent by a super user, to overide any protection which users may have put up to stop messages from the system.

This command will work in most cases. There are some application packages, however, on certain systems which block the receipt of **wall** messages. This presents problems as it obviously prevents users receiving any warning of close down.

Such packages are fortunately, at present, extremely rare. You can help make sure that they do stay rare by refusing to purchase any package which blocks **wall** messages. It is always a good idea to ask for a demonstration on your system of any package you are considering. In this case it is doubly wise to check that it will allow receipt of a **wall** message on your system.

If you already have a number of application programs on your system, check that these do allow the **wall** message to appear on your users'terminal screens. If you find any applications that block **wall** you will have to find some other way of warning all users. This may well involve you in walking round the system and telling everybody that you are about to close down. It will not hurt to inform any people on the system within earshot that you are about to close down the system, in any case.

wall should be given again as an intermediate warning.

After the warning period has expired use **wall** to announce that the system is closing down, then use the system **kill** command to kill all processes. This will return the system to the single user shell on the console.

The normal form of this command is **kill -1 1**. This sends signal 1 to process number 1, which is always **init**. You should check, however, that this signal is the correct one on your system before using it. Some configurations of **init** require other signals to return the system to single user.

The next stage is to issue the command **sync**. This will flush the main memory buffers. After issuing the **sync** command wait a sufficient time to allow all disk operations to be completed. This will vary according to which system or systems you have and the speed of the disk drives. Only then can you switch off.

Many systems are supplied with a shell script to carry out the steps detailed above, up to the issue of the **kill** command. As this will kill the shell script, any subsequent requirements have to be handled manually. If your system does not have such a shell script you can easily write one. A simple one is given below.

```
for v in 5 4 3 2 1

   do

echo "System close down in =v minutes"  | /etc/wall
   sleep 60

   done

   echo "System NOW closing down"  | /etc/wall

   kill -1 1
```

A number of reference works state that all mounted devices should be unmounted before close down. Strictly speaking this is not neccessary, but can be considered good practice. The **umount** commands should be given after **sync**.

A useful point to note is that after the **umount** command has been given, you have the ideal opportunity to carry out system support activities which need to have access to raw devices. This is especially true of procedures like backup.

If you carry out any system support activities at this time remember to issue another **sync** command to update the root file system, which is still mounted, prior to switching off the power.

5.4.1 Emergency Close Down.

There are some circumstances, fortunately not many, where it may be necessary to close down the system without going through the full close down procedure.

If you need to carry out an emergency shut down of the system, there are a number of minimum commands that you ought to carry out. Whatever else you do, you should enter the **sync** command, then power down before any more file system activity can occur. The problem with this is that if you have a slow drive on the system, the time taken to write to disk is sufficient for new processes to start up and access disks.

A more effective procedure for emergency close down is to enter the command **kill -1 1** or the appropriate version of the command for your system, and then follow this with **sync**.

Though such procedures may result in users losing some of their work due to logical inconsistencies for the application program, the file system should be relatively intact when the system is brought back up.

5.5 Mounting File Systems.

One of the friendly parts of Unix, and there are a few, is that you can temporarily add file systems to the system file hierachy at any point. This is achieved by using the **mount** command.

The directory, /, is the root directory of the system. It is also the top directory of the root file system. This file system is always mounted. All other file systems need to be mounted onto the system.

Many are mounted automatically during the **rc** process started by **init** during the transition to the multiuser state. Others, for a variety of reasons, are not. The main reasons for not mounting file systems are:

> The system contains processes you may not wish run. An example of this could be a file system containing games, which you would not want to have running during normal working hours. This file system would probably only be mounted during low system usage periods.

> A file system which contains files that have a high security aspect to them. Here, by not mounting the file system, you are making unauthorised access more difficult.

> A file system is on some form of removable media. Here you cannot mount it during the **rc** process as you cannot be certain that the removable media is on the system.

To deal with the mounting and unmounting of such file systems Unix uses the **mount** and **umount** commands. Normally these commands can be found in the directory /**etc** and they have to be called with their complete path names. It is fairly common however for suppliers to move them to the directory /**bin** so that they can be called up without the path prefix. There are points of view both for and against such a move.

To mount a file system onto a directory, you must supply the name of the device containing the file system, and the name of the directory you want it to be mounted onto.

To mount a file system which is held on a disk in the device **/dev/fp1** onto the directory **/usr/sales** the command would be:

```
/etc/mount /dev/fp1 /usr/sales
```

Note that here we have used the full name for calling the **mount** command.

The **mount** command can be invoked with no parameters, as here:

```
/etc/mount
```

The purpose of this is to list all the file-systems which are currently mounted on the system.

To unmount a file system, which must be done before a floppy disc is removed, and can be done to deny access to a file system, the command used is:

```
/etc/umount
```

To unmount the disk which was mounted in the example above, the command would be:

```
/etc/umount /dev/fp1
```

Note here that we only have to give one parameter, the name of the device which we wish to unmount.

There are, naturally, certain problems associated with **mount**.

First, on some Unix and Unix-like systems, certain commands may not perform in regard to the mounted system quite as one would expect. The only one we have direct experience of **ls - ld**, which will show the permissions on the original directory, and not those of the mounted directory. We have, however, heard of problems associated with commands like **find**. Here, again, the problem seems to be that the command recognises the permissions of the original directory and not of the mounted directory. It appears that this only happens when you have to enter the directory during a search. If the command is started from within the directory, then there are no problems.

We must emphasise that we have not experienced this, but it might be something to keep in mind. If you get unexpected problems with respect to access permissions to directories, suspect the possiblity of the command not reading the correct permissions on a mounted system.

The second problem is somewhat more serious. If a user brings a disk from another system and mounts it on your system, that disk could be used to by-pass security. It could have on it shell scripts which have the SUID (set user id) bit set and are owned by root, yet have on it execute permission for the user who has brought the disc over. It could also hold modified versions of /**bin** and **/etc**. There are also problems with files from another system having UIDs and GIDs which are not known to the system upon which they are being mounted.

It is therefore advisable for the **mount** command to be restricted to the superuser or the privileged users.

Unfortunately, there is a conflict here in that more and more applications are making increasing use of floppy disk for personal storage. The user is being expected to put disks in and remove them, meaning that the user has to mount and unmount devices. As standard application programs cannot know in advance which device is going to be used, it is often left to the user to mount his or her disk onto the system before running the application.

Here then is the conflict: for security the user must not have access to the **mount** command; for efficiency, the user needs it to run the application program. Some of the more recent application programs which require the user to mount his or her own disks have developed procedures for doing this from within the software. This is by far the best approach.

If this is not possible and users must be given some way of mounting disks, it is suggested that this should be provided from within shell scripts. Such a shell script should not only mount the disk on the required device, but also check that the disk only contains those files required for the application.

Chapter Six

System Configuration.

When your system is installed it will be configured to meet your requirements, or at least your perceived requirements, by your supplier. You may from time to time however have to adjust some aspects of this configuration. This can be done through amending certain of the system files.

6.1 Adding Devices.

Before you can add any device to the system, besides actually physically installing the device, the code to support that device must exist within the system. In some circumstances this will mean adding new device drivers to the kernel. Such actions are very system dependent and also generally require access to the system source code, which you will not have access to on most commercial systems. Should such an addition be needed, then it is generally necessary to go to your supplier.

Given that the devices are already physically installed, and presuming that the necessary driver code is present in the kernel, devices may be added to the system by making a file entry for them in the directory /**dev**.

Unix recognises two types of device. The first is the character serial device, which is a device from which characters are read, or to which characters are written, only in serial mode. Classically these are terminals, printers and tapes.

The other type of device is a block-structured device. This is a device which is divided into blocks which may be read from or written to individually, and not specifically in a serial order. To do this it is normal for the read/write head to be positioned prior to the read or write. Block-structured devices are those used for the file system and can only be accessed by ordinary users via the standard file I/O requests.

Devices are defined to the system by means of a major and a minor number. The major number is the reference to the driver in the kernel which controls that type of device. The minor number is the specific designation for that device. In the case of a disk drive the major number will refer to the disk controller driver, whilst the minor number will refer to the disk drive on the controller.

To add a new device you need to know both numbers. This might seem quite difficult. In practice it is not too bad. If you take, for example, the case of a disk drive:

-It arrives and you unpack it.

-You attach the cable that comes out of the back to one of the sockets on the disk drive controller card. This socket will be numbered, or it should be, with the minor number.

If you are lucky you will find the number assigned to the disk controller on the controller. (In all probability it will not be there, but you can find out what it should be by looking at the numbers assigned to other disk drives on the same controller. These will be listed in the directory /**dev**). That will then give you the major number.

-All you have to do now is make the entry in the directory /**dev** for the new device. Here Unix supplies the command **mknod** which normally lives in the directory /**etc**.

Note that /**etc/mknod** is addressed by its full path name. The syntax for it is:

```
/etc/mknod [device name] [type] [major number] [minor number]
```

The device name should be given in full, starting with the directory, so a new floppy disk drive might be called /**dev/fp4**.

As there are two device types, **b** for block devices and **c** for character serial devices, to add a fourth floppy disk drive onto the controller which has the major number 8, the command is:

```
/etc/mknod /dev/fp4 b 8 4
```

We now have our floppy disk drive on the system and we can use it, that is, so long as we do not want to address it in the raw state. A raw device is a character serial device, and we have just specified this device to be a block-structured device. The answer to this problem is that where you have a block-structured device you also have to make an entry for a character serial device. The convention is that this will have the same name as the block-structured device, but it is given an **r**, for raw, in front of it.

To make that addition, we write:

```
/etc/mknod /dev/rfp4 c 8 4
```

Having done all that, there is a question that might well be asked before you start any of this complex process. What are you doing adding devices yourself. You ought to keep in mind this little maxim: you pay the supplier enough, why not let him or her do it!

6.2 Amending the rc File.

During the **init** process, when the system goes multi-user, it reads and executes a file called **/etc/rc**. (See the section on system start up.)

A fairly standard version of **/etc/rc** is:

```
# Set path for commands
 PATH = /bin:/usr/bin
 # Clear the list of logged on users
 cat /dev/null > /etc/utmp
# Clear the list of mounted file-systems
cat /dev/null > /etc/utmp
 # Mount standard file systems
 /etc/mount /dev/usr /usr
 /etc/mount /dev/hd2 /usr/sales
/etc/mount /dev/hd3 /usr/accounts
 /etc/mount /dev/hd4 /adm
 /etc/mount /dev/spl /usr/spool
 /etc/mount /dev/tmp /tmp
 # Clear the /tmp directory
 rm -r /tmp/*
```

```
# Call up shell script to set date

/etc/dateset

#Start regular main memory flushing

/etc/cron

# Start cron

/etc/cron -1

# Clear printer spooler directory and set printer

/etc/prinset

fi
```

Of course, your **/etc/rc** file will not be quite the same. This example, above, has a couple of special shell scripts it calls up to do jobs many files would have to do within the file. The file systems mounted will also differ, and you will almost certainly want to carry out operations which are not included.

More importantly, it is very possible that you will either want to do things which are not included in the file supplied with your system, or not do things which are in the file.

A common example of how this can arise, is that most commercially supplied **/etc/rc** files play safe and mount every file system present on the system, at start up. This is all well and good, but in probability you will not want them all mounted. Some file systems, like **/usr/lib/games**, for example, you might prefer to keep unmounted during normal working hours.

If this is the case, use an editor and adjust the file to suit your requirements, but remember to take a copy first, just in case. On the other hand, unless you do something extremely daft, there is little real damage you can do. Even if the file fails completely, you can always issue the commands direct from the console. In any case, however, it is a good idea to have a hard copy of the file printed out.

6.3 The /etc/ttys File.

The **/etc/ttys** file contains details of which terminal lines on the system are going to be active and in what way. Each line in the file describes one terminal connection. A fairly typical line might be:

```
12tty07
```

The first character on the line is either a one or a zero.

Zero indicates to **init** that no action should be taken with respect to this line. It is not enabled for logins.

If the first character is 1, then the line is enabled for logins, and the baud rate and parity are set.

The second character gives information about the baud rate, which, basically, is the speed of transmission. This is interpreted from a table addressed by the **getty** process and differs between systems, and on some it can also indicate a type of processes. In System V Unix and Berkeley Unix it only represents the baud rate. You should consult your system information for precise details.

The remainder of the line gives the name of the device as it exists in the directory /dev.

6.3.1 The /etc/ttytype File.

On Unix System V and Berkeley Unix the file, **/etc/ttytype**, contains information about the type of terminal that is in use. The entry in each line is split into two halves. The first half contains details of the type of terminal, while the second half has the name of the terminal, as it is in the directory **/dev**.

A number of Unix-like systems have also started to adopt this approach.

Details of the terminal protocols are actually held in the file **/etc/termcap**.

Generally there should be no need to touch these files. If you have a terminal added by your supplier, then you ought to expect him or her to update the system information for you.

There are two occasions when action may have to be taken:

-When the status of a terminal line has been changed you may have to change the enable/disable entry from zero to 1 or vice versa.

-When a terminal has failed and you have to move a terminal with a different baud rate to that line.

Many systems have shell scripts for making such admendments and you should consult your system documentation for the precise details.

6.4 Enabling and Disabling Ports.

It is sometimes useful to be able to enable and disable ports so that they can only be used during specified periods. Some systems support an **enable** and **disable** command, but there is a wide variation in its implementation. Again, you should consult your system documentation for the exact information that applies.

Where you do have the **enable** command available for use with a port, the syntax is:

```
enable [device name]
```

It should be noted that in XENIX system documentation it is recommended that a full minute should be allowed to elapse between use of the command and use of the device named.

6.5 Regular Events.

Unix systems have a command which executes events on a regular basis, according to certain entries in the file **/usr/lib/crontab**.

This is **cron**.

The process **cron** is normally started up by **init** when it executes the **/etc/rc** file. If it is not on your system, change the **/etc/rc** file, as detailed above.

The **cron** process wakes up periodically, reads the **crontab** file, and if there are any commands in that file due to be executed, carries them out. If you want to alter what is going on, you need to edit the file **/usr/lib/crontab**.

Here is part of a typical example:

```
0 * * * * /bin/date > /dev/console

30 9 * * * /bin/calendar

0,10,20,30,40,50 * * * * /usr/lib/uucp/aduucp

5 10 * * * /etc/runadmin

30 17 * * * /etc/gameson

30 7 * * * /etc/gamesoff
```

If we examine this, we will find that each line in the file contains one entry which is made up itself of a number of fields. In turn, the fields themselves are in two parts. First there are the time fields, where a series of numbers are separated by spaces or an asterisk which is the wild card character for all valid values. There are five fields in this part. Secondly, the last part is a single field and is the command line.

The first of the time fields is the minute field. This can contain a value between 0 and 59. In theory you could put the wild card in here, but it is not really practicable as it would mean that the process would run every time **cron** woke up, given that the other fields were valid. That would defeat the object of **cron** somewhat.

It is possible to set the time for a number of minutes in the hour by listing them separated by commas, as here:

```
5,20,35,50
```

This example causes the command to be run on the 5th, 20th, 35th and 50th minute during any hour.

In this illustration the command **/usr/lib/uucp/aduucp** is run every ten minutes. This is a shell script which itself runs **uucico** and **uuclean** if required. In this way one entry can start a number of processes.

The next field is the hours field. In this field, the hour on which the command is to be run is specified. If it is to be run on every hour, the asterisk is used.

Going back to our example above, **/bin/calendar** is run at 9.30 am each day. If you look at the first entry you will see that the minute field is set to 0 and the hour field is left wild. This has the effect of running the command on the hour. The valid range for entries in the hour field is zero to 23.

The next field is the field for the day of month. This can have a value of 1 to 31. The way the entry works is as for the previous to fields.

There can be problems with this field if it is not correctly set. Quite often system managers require reports from system logs, accounts, or files on the system, of monthly activities. It is quite common to set an entry in **crontab** to carry out the production of these. The problem is when do you set the entry.. If you set the entry for the 31st, what happens on months which only have 30 days or in February with its 28 or 29 day?

The answer to this is to set the entry to run first thing on the morning of the first day of the month. An entry which will do this is:

```
1 0 1 * * /etc/mnthadmin
```

Here, at one minute past midnight, the system will run a shell script called **mnthadmin** which will carry out monthly reporting. This sort of entry is quite common on many systems, but should not be used if your system is not running constantly. In many small commercial systems where systems are started up and closed down each day, problems could arise when the 1st day of the month is a non-working day. In these circumstances it is better to carry out such monthly administration reporting and processes manually.

The next field is the field for the month of the year. This accepts values from 1 to 12.

Finally we have the field for the day of the week, which accepts values from 0 to 6 with Sunday being 0 and Saturday being 6. This can be very useful for making sure weekly jobs are carried out.

It should be noted that **cron** will run all programs with superuser privilege. It is often advisable, especially with file administration programs, to have them run at some lower privilege level. This can be achieved by including the **su** command in the command field of the entry, in order to change the user. The form in which it should be used is:

```
su - [name] -c [command]
```

The - argument following **su** causes the environment to be changed to that of the user on login. The **-c** argument executes the command string which follows. Therefore if we wanted to run **/usr/lib/uucp/uucio** directly we could use the command field:

```
su - uucp -c /usr/lib/uucp/uucio
```

An alternative method of running commands at a lower privilege level is to run them from shell scripts with the SUID bit set, where the shell scripts are owned by a user with a lower privilege level than **root**. This is regarded by many as the preferred approach. There is however a problem, since some systems will not reset the user identification when the user is a superuser. You will have to check out your own system to know precisely what applies to it.

Chapter Seven
Monitoring the System.

Keeping an eye on the system, making sure that it is not abused, misused or building up problems for you is an important part of the system manager's job.

Many of the difficulties which are associated with Unix and Unix- like systems can be avoided if the system is carefully monitored during operation. Monitoring can be an additionally useful aid to improving system performance. On many commercial systems where the system management has little opportunity to influence the configuration and set up of the system, only those performance related activities which arise from monitoring are available to the system manager.

7.1 Monitoring Users: the who Command.

One of the most useful tools for the system manager is the **who** command, used either directly or on the **/usr/admin/wtmp** file.

Used directly without parameters **who** will give you a list of those users who are currently logged on the system. It does this by reading the information from the file **/usr/utmp**. If you invoke the command you will be presented with a list of every user who is currently logged on the system:

```
$ who

system    console may 5   10:40

demo      tty3      may 5   10:59

nigel     tty1      may 5   11:23
```

At first sight the listing would appear to be of little use, other than finding out if somebody to whom you want to send a message is on the system, so that you can use the **write** command. Let us, however, consider a situation where the response time on the system has dropped to an unacceptable level.

Unix and Unix-like systems create processes for each user who is logged on to the system. As these users invoke application programs and commands, more and more processes are created. The more processes there are on a system the slower that system will be.

One way in which the performance of any system can be improved is to reduce the number of users who are on the system at any one time. To this end, one thing for which you should be on the look out is the permanent logon. There are, for example, users who log on to the system the moment they arrive in the office in the morning whether they need to or not, and don't log off until they leave at night. They might even fail to log off then. In system terms this is quite unacceptable. Such users should be encouraged to log on only when they actually need to use the system and to log off as soon as they have finished.

On the other hand, a proportion of your staff will use the system at frequent intervals throughout the day although they are not always working at a terminal. In such cases, logging on and logging off once a day is acceptable.

This is one area where your general approach to training will pay dividends, so that even those staff who only ever use one application have some idea of the concepts behind using a computer system. The reason why people just log on whether they need to or not is because they have only the vaguest idea of both the system they are using and the sort of demands it can meet. If this is happening, then there are faults in your training program which need to be corrected.

A useful exercise for the system manager is to obtain a list of who is logged on the system using the **who** command, then actually go round the system and find out what they are doing. If you find that they are not using the system, you can find out, diplomatically, why they are still logged on. If you treat this exercise initially as a means of evaluating your training and staff awareness, it will be very instructive. On the other hand, if you find unattended terminals, where people have gone off to a meeting or to lunch but left their terminal logged on, then you need to take rather quicker action. Merely logging them off, which is what you should do first, of course, will not solve the problem.

Although it may sound a rather obvious fault to correct, it is suprising how often you will find, especially in commercial situations, that users will leave their terminals for quite long periods of time, still logged onto the system. Indeed, you might even care to experiment by checking system performance before you start to take action over this area and after. There is a more serious element, however, to this point about logging off unused or unattended terminals. Not only are system resources wasted, with consequent degradation of system performance, but a real threat is posed to system security. Whilst your authorised person is away from the terminal, unauthorised users can obtain access to what may be very sensitive information.

A recent example of this from a software development department of all places will illustrate the point. One of the senior staff decided to run a specific procedure which he knew made heavy demands on system resources. To avoid inconveniencing other staff in the department he decided to run it one afternoon when he knew most of the staff were away at a course. He was somewhat suprised when he checked the system with the **who** command to find that nearly every member of staff was still logged onto the system. They had all gone off to the course, but most had failed to log off.

Another revealing result of physically checking who is on the system as compared with the listing given by the **who** command will be which users are allowing other parties to make use of their login, or where unauthorised users have obtained another user's password. An interesting result was obtained recently on one Unix-like system in a financial institution when the output of **who** was compared with the holiday list. It was found that nearly a quarter of the users who were logged on the system were actually away on holiday!

A further use of the **who** command is in conjunction with the file **/usr/adm/wtmp**, if it, or a similar one, is maintained on your system. Not all Unix-like systems maintain files of this type and even under Unix it is known by a number of different names. The name given here is that used on Unix version 7 and Berkeley Unix. Under System V the file is called **/etc/wtmp**. Various Unix-like systems which support this file, give their own names to it. Essentially it is a history file of logins, system booting and clock resets. If you can't find the file on your system, check with your system suppliers whether you have one and what name it has been given.

First, however, a word of warning about the **/usr/adm/wtmp** file. It is one of those files which is liable to grow large and consume disk space. This will need to be checked and kept within bounds. (See the section on disk usage.)

If you access this file you will get a set of information telling you who has logged on to the system and when the file being used was created. It also informs you at which terminal they logged in, and when the system clock has been adjusted. A fairly common format for output from this file with the **who** command is as follows:

```
$ who | usr | adm | wtmp

          console  Dec 12  16:45
          |        Dec 12  16:45
          {        Dec 14  09:40
          tty01    Dec 14  09:41
          console  Dec 14  09:41
sysman    console  Dec 14  09:48
paul      tty01    Dec 14  11:14
```

When decoded, this display of information holds the following information. First, the system was booted up with the system date reading Dec 12 and the time 16:45. This is the date and time when it was last closed down. A useful point to be made here from the security point of view is to check that this corresponds to the entry in the system log. (See the section on security.)

The next two lines, the one with the bar (|) and the one with the brace (**(**), show that the system clock has been reset, from 16:45 on December the 12th to 09:40 on December the 14th. This indicates the start up time. Next we get the information that two terminals have been made available for the system to use: **tty01** and the **console.**

The first logon recorded is that of **sysman** at 09:48. This was then followed by **paul** logging on at 11:14.

For the system manager this file can provide a great deal of information about how the system is being used. Analysis of such information is very much a matter of experience, particularly of your own system, since the variables that affect each system are so different. There are a few general aspects which you can look for though: some in the region of security (covered in more detail in the section on security), and others which are discussed here.

One thing which many systems suffer from is usage peaks. If you find that regularly at certain times the overall response time of the system is getting to a level where it is unacceptable, it is worthwhile looking to see if these correspond to usage peaks.

If upon examination of the **/usr/adm/wtmp** file you discover that most of the time only about 25% of the users are on the system, but at specific times, on a regular basis, all the users are coming onto the system, then you have a usage peak. Another type of peak is when the same number of users all start heavily system dependent operations at the same time. In such a case, it could be that when all the users are on the system they are carrying out tasks which make low demands on the system resources, but when only a few are on they are doing jobs which take up a high level of system resources. Whatever the reason, the chances are that such usage peaks will correspond to the periods of unacceptable system response time.

If you do find that you have such a correspondence, you then have to consider what steps you can take.

The first thing to do is to find out why all the users are logging onto the system at the same time. Once you find out what tasks they are performing it might be possible to reschedule some of these tasks so that they are carried out at a time of low system usage.

This can be illustrated with the example of a finance company which found it regularly had problems with response times between eleven in the morning and just after noon. Examination of the system usage showed that the system was being used most of the time for account enquiry and account updating. These did not appear to produce an unacceptable deterioration in system performance.

The system was also used, however, by the marketing department to extract account information upon which to base mail shots, and by the collection department to extract data about accounts which had gone into arrears. Both these departments ran procedures to obtain this information at about eleven each morning. It was the added demand made upon the system by these activities which brought about the unacceptable performance level.

Both the marketing and collection departments required the information they were seeking by one o'clock in the afternoon in order to get print runs completed so material could be posted by four o'clock in the afternoon. Examination of the requirements of both departments showed that they were only interested in data which had been entered during the previous working day, not in current updates. There was therefore no reason why these processes should not be run overnight, thereby avoiding the clash of demands for system resources with the account enquiry and update activities which had to take place during the day.

In this example there was an additional benefit. It now meant that the departments had their lists for nine o'clock each morning and could get the print runs completed so that they could catch the mid-day post. This resulted in a far higher percentage of the post being delivered by the next day.

Unfortunately answers are not always that easy. Sometimes you have a situation where system usage peaks cannot be avoided. You will also have situations where most of the users are logged on the system for most of the time and using the system legitimately. In both these types of cases, if you find that the system response time is becoming unacceptable you may have to consider the provision of more system resources in terms of memory, processing power and disks.

Another reason for examining the **/usr/adm/wtmp** file on a regular basis is to see if there is any change in the pattern of logins. Any such change can often be a sign of a change in demands on the system. As such it provides an early warning indicator of problems which may lie ahead. In this regard it is often useful to keep a hard copy of the file so that you can compare what is happening now with what was going on in the past.

This is very useful if you find that the performance of the system has suddenly become unacceptable but you have no apparent change in the usage of the system. Comparing the logon situation with the past can often show changes which are not immediately apparent.

7.2 Monitoring Processes: the ps Command.

There are other causes which may result in a slowing down of system response time to an unacceptable level, other than the number of users on a system and a multiplication of processes. Applications also generate processes, and some applications can place very heavy demands on system resources. It is therefore often useful to know just what processes are running on your system. This information is maintained in the kernal tables and may be accessed by means of the command **ps**.

Used by itself or with the -l argument, this command will produce a listing of processes associated with your terminal. To obtain a listing of all processes running on the system you will have to use the command line **ps -a**. Note that the options for Berkeley Unix are different.

If you do not use the -l option, for the long listing, the process status command will give you four columns of information:

```
$ ps

        PID        TTY        TIME    COMMAND

         72        01        0:18    sh
         87        01        0:02    du
        288        01        0:01    ps
```

The first column contains the Process Identification number, the PID, which is the number by which the process is known to the system. In the second column you will find the number of the terminal from which the process has been called. This is followed by the elapsed time for the process. In the fourth column is the command which called up the process.

The PIDs 0 and 1 are reserved for special system processes.

A more informative listing of information can be obtained by making use of the -l option to give a long listing. To get this listing, for all processes on the system, you will have to use an additional argument, which varies with system. On System V it is the -e option. The format for such listings also varies according to the type of system you are on.

A typical example is:

F	S	UID	PID	PPID	C	PRI	NI	ADDR	SIZE	WCHAN	TTY	TIME	CMND
1	S	22	35	1	0	32	20	40	33	child	01	0:24	sh
1	R	22	204	35	14	48	20	5d	59		01	0:01	ps

Here you have quite detailed information displayed about all the processes which are running on the system. The first field, headed F, gives the octal value of the process flag. These values are additive, which means you add the relevant values together. In this case, if it is a process in core, it has the flag 01 and if it is also a system process, it has the flag 02 as well. Thus the total flag will be 03.

The different octal flag values are:

01	in core
02	system process
04	locking in core
10	being swapped
20	being traced by another process

The next column gives us the state of the processes, these are:

S	sleeping
W	waiting
R	running
I	intermediate
Z	terminated
T	stopped

Next we come to the column headed UID, this gives the User Identification number of the process owner. It is followed in the next column, which is headed PID, by the Process Identification number.

If the process is a child we find in the next column the Parent Process Identification number.

The next column, headed CPU, gives the value which is assigned to this particular process for scheduling. This is followed in the next column by the priority of the process. The higher the number given in the PRI column the lower the priority of the process.

Next is a column headed NICE (or NI, or even N). This gives the number set by either the system default or the NICE command and is used in priority computation.

If the process is in memory, the next column, headed ADDR or similar, will hold the address of the process in memory. Otherwise the address given here will be its address on disk.

The next column gives the size of the process. This is followed by a column headed WCHAN. If a process has requested a system resource and that resource is not available then the process must wait until the resource becomes available. The resource it is waiting for is listed as an address in this field. If the process is running, this field will be blank.

The terminal from which the process is controlled is listed in the column headed TTY.

As would seem logical, the column headed TIME gives the elapsed time for the process. The final column is the command column, normally headed something like CMD, and gives the command which invoked the process.

The question, of course, is what use all this information can be to the system manager. It must be admitted that in general it will not be all that much. It can be of tremendous interest to a Unix freak or system specialist.

There are a few times, however, when it can be useful. The first will be when the performance of the system becomes unacceptably low while there are few users on the system. It can then be useful to have a look to see exactly what processes are running. It may be that there are many background processes running which are taking up a large volume of system resources. If there are not and the level of processes running should be well within the capacity of the system you will have to look for other explanations for the drop in performance.

Another reason for looking at the **ps** listing is to find a specific process. If a user has made an error in entering a command, he or she can easily lock up a device or a terminal with a looped process. Alternatively a long process which is also very demanding in terms of system resources may have been started by a user at a time when it is not acceptable for that process to be run on the system.

In such cases it will be necessary for you to kill the process. To do this you must have the process identification number, which you can obtain easily using **ps**.

If you find upon examining the listing that a large proportion of processes are waiting for the same system resource, check to make sure that there are no problems with that resource.

7.3 Killing Processes.

If a system is being slowed down unacceptably by an overwhelming number of processes and you cannot reduce the number by getting users to log off, then some of them will have to be removed. Similarly, if a process has been invoked in error, or has locked up a terminal or device, you will have to remove it.

The way to do this is via the Unix command **kill**, which is why such a procedure is known as killing. The syntax for the command is:

```
kill [process identification number]
```

To kill a process, therefore, which has the PID of 75: the command line is:

```
$ kill 75
```

This will send a software termination signal to the process which has the PID of 75. Normally this will kill that process.

Sometimes the process cannot be killed with the standard signal that is sent, which is 15. In that case, one of the other termination signals must be sent. The normal ones to try are either 3, the quit signal, or 9 the sure kill signal.

As **sigkill** cannot be caught or ignored it is ususally known as the sure kill signal. To use this you have to specify the following parameter to the **kill** command:

```
$ kill -9 [PID]
```

7.4 Disk Space.

One of the main advantages of the Unix operating system which made it so popular in universities and software development environments is its highly flexible and dynamic file structure. This means that files can expand and contract as and when required. Unfortunately there seems to be an unwritten law in computing that files will only expand, until they fill the disk space available for them.

With Unix, of course, they can even expand beyond this, and with no warning you can find yourself running out of disk space.

The system manager must constantly check that the amount of disk space available is sufficient at all times to meet the demands which may be made on the system. Unfortunately with new systems it is very difficult to predict what these demands are going to be. Dealers tend to give general figures which seem to be based on the following calculation:

- 256 Kbytes of main memory.

- Plus 256 Kbytes for each terminal

- Plus 5 Mbytes of basic disk storage

- Plus another figure of basic disk storage for each terminal.

It has been observed that they tend to adjust this final figure at will, to suit what they think they can sell to the purchaser, or what they have in stock at the time.

In general the disk capacity of most systems upon installation is not adequate for the demands which will be placed on the it. This is partly due to the fact that most users severely underestimate the amount of disk usage which will be generated, even where the users are experienced in dealing with Unix.

There are also estimated to be some fifteen percent of new installations where the disk capacity provided is far in excess of what the system needs or can be envisiged as needing. Although this does represent a loss of money, and probably somewhat higher running expenses, it is not as bad as having too little disk space.

7.4.1 Disk Usage.

You can find out details of how a disk is being used with the Unix command **du**. The syntax of this command is:

```
du [option] [directory]
```

This command has two standard options available on most Unix type systems: **-s** and **-a**. **-s** reports on the total number of blocks used. **-a** reports on the total size of each ordinary file as well as the number of blocks used. Under version 7 and System V Unix from AT&T there is also a **- r** option which reports certain error conditions. It should be noted that the **-a** and **-s** options are mutually exclusive.

It should be noted that for the normal user there is a limitation to the use of **du** in that the file size is obtained by reading the files. The user is therefore only informed about files for which he or she has read access rights. Whilst this is perfectly acceptable for the user who wants to know how large his or her file systems are, it is not acceptable to the system manager who needs to know about all the files on the system. To get this information the command must be called up in superuser mode.

The **du** command is one which is commonly used by system managers and is therefore an ideal one to include in a shell script with the SUID bit and execute permission for group both set.

To find the usage on any specific disk you should start from the root directory on that disk.

A fairly typical output would be:

```
  $ du /usr/sales
125     /usr/sales/admin
15      /usr/sales/closed
1276    /usr/sales/customers
8238    /usr/sales/accounts
674     /usr/sales/letters
38      /usr/sales/dates
10166   /usr/sales
```

An important thing to note about this is that the total number of blocks used is less than the total given for each sub-directory. The reason for this is that if you have a number of files in one sub-directory which are linked to another sub-directory, the blocks in those files will be counted in each sub-directory, but only once in the total.

In this case the files containing customers' names and addresses existed in the accounts sub-directory, but were linked to the customer sub-directory. As a result the two hundred blocks involved appear in both calculations, but only as two hundred blocks in the total.

The main use for the **du** command is to find out how large a specific file system or section of it is. In such cases you would start from the parent directory of the tree within the file system that you wanted information on in terms of its disk usage.

7.4.2 Disk Free Space.

To find out how much disk space you have free on any device the command to use is **df**. This command can be invoked either without giving arguments, with a device name as the argument, or, on some systems, the mounted name of the device.

If no argument is given, a default file-system list is used to check on all mounted devices. This does not apply to all systems, and you have to check your system documentation.

The output from **df** is given normally as a list of the number of free blocks available on the device. Here a word of warning is necessary, since with a number of utilities on some Unix and Unix-like systems you will get this report based on the concept of a 512 byte block, even though your file system is using a different block size. You should check your system information with reference to **du**, **df** and **quot** on this point.

With Unix version 7 and System V there are two options which can be invoked with **df**. The first is the **-t** option which reports the total number of allocated blocks and inodes as well. The **-f** option causes **df** to count the number of blocks in the free block list.

7.4.3 Available Disk Space.

Here we start to get into a difficult area, as the question about how much disk space you should keep available is difficult to answer. There are many different arguments about this. One thing that is becoming increasingly obvious, however, is that the guidelines which have grown up over the last few years in academic and development environments are not applicable to the commercial world. Generally in the commercial world you cannot afford to run out of disk space, so you need to provide additional free disk space, over and above what has been regarded as acceptable in non-commercial environments.

There is a wide spread opinion amongst system managers that you should keep somewhere in the region of 25 to 30 percent free disk space available on your system. This is an acceptable guideline in most cases. What is important is to make sure that you maintain adequate free space on all devices.

On a commercial system it is not standard practice to write new commands and add them to the command directories. This means that the free space on the devices which hold these directories can be fairly low. On the other hand, many application programs produce temporary files to a quite extraordinary degree. They also seem to have a heavy disposition to producing log files of activities. These can quickly expand to eat up disk space.

You should examine your system carefully and make an assessment of probable disk usage per device. Make regular re-examinations to update your assessment, as things can change. Use this as a basis for setting a safty margin for each device. On those devices which hold only the command files, this might be quite low, but we would suggest not less than 10 per cent. On heavily used devices, such as those holding temporary or log files, the figure should be relatively high, and about 35 per cent.

7.4.3.1 What to do about Disk Space Shortage.

Should the level of disk space available fall below the safty margin you have set, the first thing to do is warn all users to be careful when working on that device. Next you have to make some more disk space available to them.

See first if there are any files on the device which can be removed. Initially look for system generated files, log files and old temporary files which have not been cleared out. Look out too for system hoggers. These are users who build up large file systems by the simple expedient of never clearing them out. If you are working on a Version 7, a Berkeley Unix system, or on some Unix-like systems, you will have the command **quot** on your system. This is a very useful tool for the system manager. It will provide a breakdown of disk space usage, by user.

The syntax for the command is:

```
quot [ option ] [ filesystem ]
```

There are three options available in most versions of **quot**, though only one is of general use. Some versions on Unix-like systems only support this option:

```
-f
```

This will give you a count of the number of files owned by each user, in addition to the number of blocks.

As it is not a generally used command, the **quot** command is normally held in the directory /etc and so should be addressed by its full name.

If no file system is specified, **quot** takes the default file list, see **df**, and operates on the whole file system.

A typical output from **quot** would be:

```
$ /etc/quot /dev/root
/dev/root
4768  root
868   sys
678   adm
186   bin
31    uucp
7     mlxm
```

If you find when you get a report form **quot** that a particular user has a far larger file usage than expected, examine those files carefully. Find out if that user is being wasteful and hogging files.

One thing you should look out for when using **quot** is files which have a number instead of a user name. This occurs when you have a file on the system which has a UID for the file owner which does not match up with any entry in the password file.

There are two main reasons for such occurences. First, the user who owned the file has been removed from the system, but the file has not been deleted. (See section on deleting users.) The other reason is that when files are moved between systems, the ownership of the file may not have been reset to its new owner. In such cases it will have the ownership set to a UID for a user on the originating system.

Where you find such files, try to find out who is using them so that ownership can be assigned. It is often found that a threat to delete all unclaimed files after seven days will result in a number of such files being claimed.

You may find that after removing all the dead files, and the temporary files, together with any other files you can get off the system, you still have not made up sufficient space. In such cases the next step is to see if you can move sections of the file system to other devices which are not so heavily used.

Finally you should consider purchasing more disk storage space. This generally is the answer sooner or later.

7.5 Problems with the Swap Area.

If you are having problems with the swap area, you may need legal advice! That might be a bit drastic, but there should really be no problems. The swap area should be set up by the supplier when the system is configured initially.

If you do have problems, then you should contact your system supplier to sort them out, as normally they will require some form of system re-configuration to solve them.

There is one important point,however: *dump all files first*. Nearly every adjustment of the swap area is going to involve a re-configuration of the whole file system. You must make backup copies of the file system before you start doing this or allowing anybody else to undertake it.

Chapter Eight
System Performance.

In general terms, there is not all that much that a system manager can do to improve the performance of a commercial Unix or Unix-like system. Such work really requires a high level of knowledge and is a job for a system specialist. It also requires access to source code.

There are a few fields, however, where modifications can be made to the system which can improve the performance to a limited extent, and which do not require a high level of system skill to implement.

8.1 The Sticky Bit.

The *sticky bit* is the last of the twelve access bits of a file. If this bit is set, the system will try to keep an image of the file in core after the process has terminated.

This can be useful particularly with frequently used commands, as it results in a reduction of swapping activity between disk and main memory and a consequent increase in speed of access to the command. This is due to the fact that when the command is called an image of it is more likely to be still in memory rather than the command having to be loaded again from disk.

The *sticky bit* for any file can be set by using the **-t** option with the command **chmod**:

```
$ chmod -t /etc/login
```

There are inevitably problems connected with such an action. First you have to decide on which commands to set the sticky bit and secondly how many commands you will treat in this way.

One file which frequently has its sticky bit set is the command **login**, though this is not really because it increases system performance. It is usually purely a cosmetic exercise. If the sticky bit of the **login** command is set, then the image is more likely to be in memory when a user logs in. This will result in a speeding up of the login process, giving users a quick response to their initial approach to the system. There is a certain amount of psychology involved here because in practice if users get a quick response at login many system managers find that they are less likely to complain about poor response times when running applications. Anything that helps settle the user into dealing with the system properly is to the benefit of the work to be done - and the system manager!

It is only worthwhile setting the sticky bit on those programs, files and commands which are being constantly accessed. You will have to study your own system. Make a list of those files most frequently called and decide yourself from that list which to set the sticky bit on. There is a certain amount of trial and error involved here and you will have to exercise some judgment. There is no point, for instance, in setting the sticky bit on a command which is always performed in the background mode, as any benefit would not be noticed.

Be careful, too, not to set the sticky bit on too many programs. If you do, you will find that the system will be reluctant to swap anything out of memory. As a result of this performance will drop and any benefit which might have been gained will be negated.

8.2 Directory Reorganisation.

Reorganising your directories is not always helpful, but can be on those systems which do not use a hash table for directory access. Berkeley systems and some Unix-like systems use hash tables: much more efficient than the direct access method used on other systems.

The basic situation is that once the system finds the correct directory for a file, it then starts to search that directory to find the right file. As it starts from the begining of the directory and works its way through to the end, the nearer the start of the directory that a file is, the quicker it will be found, and therefore the quicker the system response will be.

It therefore makes sense to organise directories so that files which have to be frequently accessed are near the start of the directory and less used files towards the end.

The way to produce such a directory is first to create a new temporary directory. Then you must copy the files from the original directory into the new directory, copying them one at a time in the order in which you want them to appear in the new directory. Once all the files have been copied across, remove the original directory and rename the new directory with the old directory's name.

Be careful when carrying out this procedure. If the system goes down whilst you are carrying it out, you may find that essential commands are not available when you try and bring the system up. Also remember that you will have to address commands by their full path name once you have moved them over to the temporary directory.

It is recommended that you only undertake re-organisation at times when the system is in single user mode. There is less chance when in that mode of the system going down due to the action of another user. You should also have done a complete system backup before starting to carry out such a re- organisation.

8.3 Minimising Disk Head Movement.

This is a much more technical matter than anything above, but something which is still well within the capabilities of a system manager. The problem is that, basically, far more time is actually taken up with the disk head moving about trying to find files or data than is taken up actually transferring data from disk to memory. If you take even a single disk, a file's data blocks will be scattered throughout the disk in very many different locations. In reading the file the disk head will have to move backwards and forwards about the disk trying to find the data blocks which compose the file. There is a further factor which causes excessive disk head movement, because the head will also be accessing the inode block to find the address of the relevant data blocks. As the inode area is at the start of the disk, which is the outermost extremity, it is not unusual to find that the disk head is having to make a significant number of movements across the full width of the disk.

Under Unix a large disk can be divided into a number of 'virtual disks'. A virtual disk is part of the whole physical disk. It is called 'virtual' because Unix treats this smaller area of the whole disk as a completely separate device, so it is virtually a disk in itself. Each of these virtual disks will have its own super-block, inode list and data-blocks. The relative amount of disk head movement which will be needed to read a file on a 'virtual disk' will be much less than would be required to read the same file if the whole of the large disk was being used, because all the relevant data is confined to a smaller area on the physical disk's surface, this is illustrated in Figure 1. It is therefore advisable when you have large capacity physical disks to divide them into smaller 'virtual disks'. This will normally be done for you when the system is supplied. If you have a single large capacity physical disk which has not been divided into 'virtual disks' you should discuss this with your supplier.

Figure 1 *Comparative Disk Head Movements for Physical and Virtual Devices*

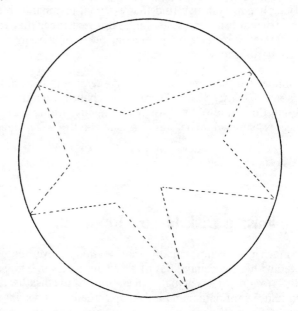

Physical Disk Head Movement

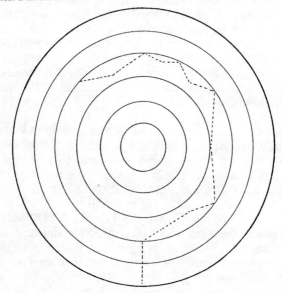

Virtual Disk Head Movement

The placing of file systems on the 'virtual disks' can, however, make a contribution to improving the performance of your system. To get the best out of such a set up, file systems which are subject to heavy traffic should be placed on 'virtual disks' which are themselves placed about the middle of the physical disk.File systems with low levels of traffic should be placed on 'virtual disks' which are situated at either the inner or the outer extremity of the physical disk.

8.4 Other Performance-Related Activities.

There are a number of other actions you can take to improve the performance of the system. For example, you can set the 'skew' factor when setting up file systems, vary system parameters, and select specific disk drives for certain operations. All these, however, require more detailed knowledge of the way the system operates that can be expected of the average commercial system manager.

More significantly, they often take considerable effort in terms of work hours to implement effectively. On a cost-efficient analysis, it might well be cheaper to add on extra memory, thereby reducing the need for swapping, or buy more disk storage with faster access speeds.

Chapter Nine

Security.

Unix, as we have said, is a very powerful operating system. It was designed to provide an easy environment for program development. This it does. It was not designed to provide a high level of security. This is does not do.

Having said that, if properly managed, the security protection that is available under Unix is acceptable for most commercial applications, and considerably better than that found on many single user operating systems.

First of all, we need to discuss what we mean by security, as the term is often used to cover two slightly different concepts. It can mean protecting files on the system from access by unauthorised parties, and preventing damage to the system by unauthorised parties. It can also mean the protection of the system from damage caused by authorised users who are just making a mess of things.

In this section we are considering security only in the former meaning. If you are having problems with careless, ignorant or difficult users we suggest you read the chapter on training or write a good set of shell scripts to coddle them.

9.1 Types of Security.

There are two ways in which you can make any computer system secure. The first way is to take steps to prevent unauthorised access to the system. The classic example of this is the locked and guarded computer room, to which programmers are not even allowed access.

This sort of approach was all well and good in the days of batch processing mainframes. With today's multi-user desk top computers, it is outmoded and impractical.

The alternative approach is to do away with physical locks and guarded rooms, and substitute a different approach. This reduction in physical control is compensated for by the use of software security checks.

It is this latter approach that Unix has adopted. It should be noted that although this method, using password files, permissions, log files and encryption, will provide adequate security for most needs, it will not stop the determined unauthorised user. It is doubtful, however, whether any protection or security method would manage that anyway.

9.2 Permissions.

Incorrectly set file permissions are one of the main causes of breaches in system security. There are a few simple rules which, if followed, will greatly increase the overall level of security.

The first step is to make sure that system command files have their permissions set to either 771 or 775. The former is used for binary programs, while the latter is used for shell scripts. Both these settings deny the normal user write permission to the files. The setting 771 can also be used for shell scripts, where there is no need for the user to have read permission.

The setting 771 gives read, write and execute permissions to the owner and the owner's group and execute permission to others. 775 gives the same permissions to the owner and group but execute and read permission to others.

If you are on a system where a privileged user group has not been used (see the section on the superuser) then there is no need to give privileged access level to members of the superuser's group. In this case you should set the permissions to 751, or 711, whichever is appropriate.

Another important point is to ensure that all system commands are owned by **root**.

While dealing with ownership by **root**, there should be no file on the system which is owned by **root** and has public write permissions. Such an arrangement is asking for trouble.

9.2.1 Permissions on Directories.

Unix directories are a special kind of Unix file, so they also have permissions. Here, though, the execute permission has a different meaning and is known as a search permission.

A directory must have search permission to enable the user to access a file which has that directory in its pathname.

It should be noted that search permission on a directory is distinct and different from read permission. The read permission allows the contents of a directory to be displayed, as when the command **ls** is used.

The effects that different permissions can have on a directory are important.

First of all, there is write permission. If any users have write permission they can add files to, or remove files from, a directory. One way in which security is sometimes broken is if amended command programs have been inserted into the command directories. For this reason the write permissions should be strictly limited on these directories.

It is a common practice among system managers to put certain files in directories on which there is public execute permission but no public read permission. At first sight this might seem strange. It does however have the advantage of effectively hiding the files. If a user wants to list the contents of a directory, he or she is denied access and cannot find out what files are held in that directory. Should they know the full path name to one of those files though, they can access it. This type of approach is specifically useful with respect to files which are only accessed from within applications, where only the application holds the full pathname of the file.

9.2.2 The SUID Permission.

The aim of most people trying to obtain unauthorised access to a computer system is to obtain superuser status. Once they get this, even for a few minutes, they are in a position to set other routes for further access at the same level.

One popular method of accomplishing superuser access was to find a **root** owned file which has the SUID bit set and has a shell escape facility. This is a command in the program which allows the user to escape from the program environment to the shell.An illustration of this is the ! command in the editor, **vi**.

What this gains is that if such a program has set the user's identification to that of the superuser, when an escape is made to shell the person making that escape will have superuser status.

The answer to this problem where you have any program on the system which has an escape to shell facility within it, is that it should not be owned by the superuser. If for any reason there is no way to avoid having a superuser-owned program with an escape to shell in it, then you should ensure that the escape to shell is preceded by a reset of the user identification. On a system where you have access to the source code this is not too much of a problem, since you can amend the source code. Unfortunately, on many commercial systems you do not have copies of the source code for your commands. In such cases it is a matter of complaining to your supplier. If your supplier will not amend the code then you should think about removing the program from the system, or denying use of the program to normal users.

Going a stage further, a more sophisticated way of obtaining superuser status is via a trapdoor.

No matter how attractive it is as an idea, this is not a small hinged flap on the back of your computer. To think of it like that is a useful way of remembering what it is, however, because it is the software equivalent and it is carefully hidden. In its basic form a trapdoor is a program put onto a system by the user which has the SUID bit set and is **root** owned. This allows the user to become a superuser. Such trapdoors can generally be spotted by the fact that there is a **root** owned SUID file in a user directory.

More complicated, and more difficult to spot, are amended versions of standard files. In this case, users take a standard command which is **root** owned and has the SUID bit set. They replace this in the directory with a version of the same command but one which allows an exit into the superuser mode, if an extra option is given. Once these are installed on a system the user can become a superuser at will, no matter how often the superuser password is changed. As the file is in one of the command directories it means there is no incriminating evidence in the users'own directories.

Finding trapdoors of this kind can be difficult. The only sign that they are there is the difference in file size between the new and original, and the different modification time.

Quite often, though, even these factors are hidden. Skillful programming will result in a modified file which is the same length as the original. The evidence of the modification time can be amended by use of the **touch** command which can reset the modification date.

One security measure which can be taken is to maintain a master copy of the system commands on removable media which is then stored in a safe place. Periodically checks can be made to ensure that the contents of the command files on the system match those master copies.

One significant point here is to make sure that the utility which you are using to do the comparison, normally **diff**, for ASCII files (shell scripts), or **cmp**, for binary files, is on the master disk. In one case where this process was used it was found that the copy of the utility in the command directories on the system had itself been amended. The result of the admendment was that no differences were reported if the files involved were in directory /**bin**.

9.2.3 Access to Special Files.

In Unix, devices such as disks and terminals are treated as a type of file. These files are contained in the directory /**dev** and are known as special files. In common with all Unix files they have a set of permission bits, which allow access to the files.

The use of special files makes the user interface to Unix much simpler than it might be otherwise. There is only one mechanism needed to handle both normal files and system devices. Unfortunately this advantage is somewhat offset by the fact that three types of special files, memory, disk and terminals, can compromise the security of the system if public access to them is allowed.

9.2.4 Access to Raw Disk Devices.

Under no circumstances should there be any direct access to the raw disk device for the normal user. Such access would enable the user directly to access the information on the disk via the inodes, thereby bypassing the security of the file access permissions.

Should it be necessary for the user to have use of a command which accesses a raw device, this should be done via a shell script which sets the SUID bit to that of the owner, who should be somebody with access to the raw device.

9.2.5 Access Directly to Memory.

For the same reason there should be no direct access to the devices /**dev**/**mem** and /**dev**/**kmem**. If such access were given, the user could obtain access to information and data, by carrying out direct reads from memory, or, worse still, amend system information by direct writes to memory.

9.2.6 Access to Terminals.

Users should not be allowed read permissions for terminals upon which they are not logged. Such a permission will allow them to intercept data which is entered at the keyboard.

There is also a problem when there is a write permission to a terminal by someone who is not actually logged on to that terminal. Some terminals can be instructed to retransmit information. In such a case a user could send a message to a terminal, and the terminal could then re-transmit that message to the system. In such a case the message would appear to the system to have originated at the terminal from which it was re- transmitted, and therefore appear to belong to the user at that terminal. If the user has superuser status, this can mean that a major breach in security hs been allowed to develop.

It is generally considered best therefore if there are no public permissions on terminals.

9.3 External Access.

The whole question of external access is starting to be a major area of concern for the modern commercial user. More and more executives and other staff are starting to work at home, or in locations away from the main site. They expect to be able to access the main computer or their department computer over a telephone line. This requires the computer installation, in turn, to have dial-up lines.

There are a number of problems associated with this. The first one is finishing a session properly. It is often said that you can terminate a session simply by hanging up the phone. In theory this is fine, but in practice it can cause problems. Sometimes a session will fail to terminate and then the next person to dial in will be able to pick up that session.

Some communications software gets round this by timing gaps between input and output. If there is an excessive gap between the last output and some input, it presumes that contact has been broken and terminates the session.

Another problem is that of unauthorised users gaining access through a dial-up line. In such situations they are in a far better position for trying to break a password. One way around this is to use call-back systems, where after the user has identified him or herself to the system, the system calls them back on a telephone number which is kept on file in the system.

Although such procedures greatly improve security, they can be circumvented.

One thing which is quite important on dial up lines is that the login program should count the number of incorrect logins that a user makes. Should these exceed a certain number, normally three, it should then take steps to prevent that user logging in. This can be done in two ways.

The first, and the way generally regarded as the safest, is to deactivate the terminal line. This can, however, cause problems for organisations which have a lot of field staff who are reporting in over the dial up line. In such cases the alternative is to deactivate the user. This is done by calling up a shell script to write a NO LOGON entry into the password entry in the user account of the file **passwd**.

9.4 Encryption.

The provision of the **crypt** facility on Unix and Unix-like systems provides means of encrypting files to a fairly acceptable level of security. It is at least safe enough for it to be advisable for any sensitive information on your system to be stored in an encrypted form.

The basic algorithom used by **crypt** implements in software a simplified version of the German 'Enigma' machine. Somewhat different versions are used on systems within the USA and those outside, apparently as a result of pressure from the CIA. What must always be borne in mind is that anything which is encryted can eventually be decrypted by a crypto-analyst given enough material and time. The aim of encryption is not therefore to prevent somebody from decrypting it by crypto-analysis, but to ensure that to do so would take so long that any benefit is wiped out.

In addition to sensitive information on the system itself, any files which are being transmitted over telephone lines, or by other means, should, in these days of highly sophisticated bugging devices, be encrypted.

The syntax for using **crypt** is:

```
crypt < clearfile > codefile
```

This requires you to give as the input file a text file to be encoded, and the name of a file into which to put the coded output.

When this has been entered, **crypt** will then ask for a key with which to encode the clearfile. This can be any string that you like to enter. All that you have to do is remember the key so that when you want to decode the file you can do so!

To decode the file the command parameters are reversed.

```
crypt < codefile > clearfile
```

or, if you want to display the file on the screen:

```
crypt < codefile
```

You should always use this version of the command to check that encryption has takem place correctly and that you did not make a mistake when entering the key, for example, before you remove the original clear file.

Some versions of **crypt** will allow the entry of the key in the command line. In these cases the command will be:

```
crypt key < clearfile > codefile
```

To encode a file:

```
crypt key < codefile
```

To display decoded file on screen and to produce a decoded file from a coded file:

```
crypt key < codefile > clearfile
```

The method used by **crypt** has been published and much has been written about it. Although it provides adequate security for most commercial purposes, if you have anything which is of a highly sensitive nature you may want to think about using a more sophisticated method for encryption.

There are also problems with entering the key as a parameter to the command. It is, for a start, visible on the terminal, as opposed to the case where **crypt** asks for the key. This does have the advantage, though, that you can see what you are typing in. A further problem is that it will be visible for a short while in the output from the **ps** command.

9.5 Passwords.

Passwords are looked at in the section on adding users to the system. However it is such an important area for system security that it will also be covered here, though this time from the security point of view, examining some of the background factors.

Unix takes a somewhat different approach to passwords from most multi-user systems. On other systems you will find that the passwords are contained in a secret file, access to which is restricted. There are advantages to this when it comes to users forgetting their passwords, or for checking that users have sensible passwords. It does however pose the problem that once somebody gets access to the file they have access to all the passwords on the system.

The Unix approach is to keep the passwords in encrypted form in a file which can be read by everybody. In fact due to the way that the file is used by the system, it has to have general read access on it.

This file, /etc/passwd, is the only place on the system where the passwords are stored. Unlike other multi-user systems, if the user forgets the password, there is no way you can go and look it up.

There are a number of ways in which the password security can be attacked, but there is no point in you, as system manager, making it easier for them. A most important rule is never set up user accounts in the password file with null passwords. This practice is often done in academic establishments at the start of each term when there are many new users. The problem is that anybody can come along and scan the password file to find a unprotected login name, then they can use it.

The most common way users try to get round password protection is by trying to guess it. This may be on a simple trial and error method: keep entering possible passwords until one works. Alternatively, it may be based on the educated guess principle, backed up with as much other information as can be gleaned in any particular situation. One of the authors of this book, who is a trained touch typist and can read hand movements over keyboards fairly accurately, has broken a number of superuser passwords by the simple expedient of getting part of the password from watching it being typed in, then guessing the rest. On one occasion, the fact that one of the superusers was actually using the password, *password*, did make breaking the password protection a good deal easier.

The message is to be on your guard!

Let us look at this question from the opposite point of view. There are problems for any user trying this type of approach. First there is a time factor. The login process is not fast, in fact many are intentionally slow to try and discourage this sort of activity. Also a number of logon programs keep a record of any unsuccessful logons. Such a record can be used to keep a check whether any attempt is being made to get onto the system in this way.

If a user is on the system, but wants to obtain another user's password, and it is normally the superuser's, he or she might try a variation on the above scheme. Here you encrypt a word and compare the result with the entry in the password file. If the two match the password has been found. Fortunately this approach is not all that effective on most Unix-like systems for two reasons. First the time taken to carry out the encryption normally makes it impractical. A second factor is the salt string which is used to modify the Data Encryption Algorithm, that encodes the password. This salt string is generated from the current system time and the process identification number. As it is very unlikely that the **pid** and system time are likely to be the same, even when the program receives the correct password the encryption will vary.

One technique which is often used for getting passwords, especially the superuser's, is a fake login. Here the user writes an application program which presents the screen image of the login prompt. This is run on a terminal and the terminal is then left for users to try to login. When they do, their password is requested as if following the normal procedure. Any password entry is then written to a file to be read later. The program gives an incorrect login response and exits, which leaves the legitimate user to log on again, this time with the real login. The owner of the fake program, however, can now log on with that user's password on file.

The giveaway that this type of deceit has taken place is that the user is required to login again. If users find this happening to them and are certain that they have logged in correctly, then you should start to suspect that you have a password thief on your system. The other approach that you can adopt, is never login as superuser. It is the superuser password which thieves are usually trying to get. Instead you can use the **su** command to change to superuser form a normal logon.

9.6 Mounted Disks.

One problem with Unix is that it accepts the contents of any mounted file system as being accurate. This has the result that if a user mounts a file system which contains copies of system commands, modified so that special permissions are not required, they can be run from the mounted disk.

One example of this was when a user mounted a disk which contained a copy of the **su** command but one which did not ask for the password. Once this was on the system, he was able to change to **root** with no difficulty. As has been said before, access to the **mount** command should therefore be strictly controlled.

9.7 Policing System Security.

One of the first items to keep an eye on is the **sulog**. This log contains a record of every use of the **su** command. In fact, some go further and keep a record of every command issued by any user after invoking **su**. If you find anybody unexpectedly changing to superuser, you have problems. Do not rely on this completely as it is within the power of the superuser to modify the **sulog**. Any competent user who breaks the system could be expected to do this at least.

It is worthwhile keeping a record of all files on the system which are owned by **root** and have the SUID bit set. Any user who breaks into the system as the superuser is likely to want to maintain a means of entry. The existence of a shell script which will allow such a person to escape as **root**, would be an easy way onto the system in future. You can check for such programs using the **find** command.

```
$ find / -perm 0004000 -user root -print
```

This command will find all files with the SUID bit set and owned by **root**. The results should be compared with your list. If there are any that should not be there, you will be able to start asking questions.

Even if there are none extra it is worthwhile checking to make sure they have not been modified to provide a trapdoor.

Another good idea is to use the **who** command regularly just to find out who is on the system. It can be quite a shock if you should find you are already logged on as superuser at another terminal!

As the **who** command gives you details of the terminal being used, you can physically go over and apprehend whoever is responsible.

If you find that the system has been broken into, you have quite a job on your hands. The only way you can really make the system secure again is to re-install it from secure masters.

9.8 Security Monitoring and the /usr/adm/wtmp File.

Monitoring the security of your system is a vital element in your role as system manager. One particular help you have is the information contained in the file **/usr/adm/wtmp**. This file, which was discussed in the section on system monitoring (mainly from the point of view of performance) is also very important when considered within the viewpoint of system security.

First it should be noted that this file is known under different names on different systems. The name given above is that found under Unix version 7. On system V it is called **/etc/wtmp**. Other Unix-like systems assign different names to it and some systems unfortunately do not have it at all. If you can't find it on your system, consult your system suppliers. It is a fairly vital part of the system, and it should be there.

Given that you have the file on your system, the points to be aware of are discussed here.

First of all you should examine the file for any incidences of the system being booted up or closed down which are not recorded in the system log book. Remember that you should be keeping a written log of everything that goes on on the system. What is important here is that on most systems anybody who carries out an IPL obtains access to the system in single user mode and therefore has superuser privileges. There can of course be good reasons why an IPL was not recorded in the log, but if you find evidence of an unrecorded IPL, you should make sure you find out why it was unrecorded.

The next thing which should be looked for is users who are logged on the system at times when you would not expect them to be present. For instance if you find that the chief accountant is apparently logging onto the system at eleven each evening, when you know she always catches a five o'clock train home, then you have a right to be suspicious, and should act upon that suspicion.

Unexpected logons can often be a sign that somebody has found another user's password and is using it to gain unauthorised access to the system. Alternatively such logons can be a sign that an authorised user is undertaking unauthorised activities and is logging on at times when he or she is not observed.

Another sign which should cause concern is when a user's level of logons increases over a very short period of time and there is no apparent change in their system activities. For instance, if a user in sales has been logging on twice a day to enter the sales invoices for the past two years and then suddenly the level of logons increases to six a day, then there might be something wrong. At the very least you need to find the reason.

There are a number of legitimate explanations why there should be such an increase in logons. First the users' work may have changed and they have to make far more use of the system. Alternatively they may have altered their working procedures. In this case, the user in sales might have decided that rather than let the sales invoices pile up throughout the morning and afternoon so he had large batches to enter, it might be easier if they were entered as they came in, a few at a time.

However such increases in usage can also indicate that a user is misusing the system. It may be that they may have suddenly found the games directory, or are trying to break somebody's password. More pertinently, it can mean that somebody has found another user's password and is getting access to the system as that user.

It is wise to keep an eye open for users who are logged in at more than one terminal at once. There are quite often legitimate reasons for somebody logging on at two terminals. It is sometimes a sign that somebody is using another user's logon identity.

A further point which should be watched for is users who are logging in from unexpected terminals. If you find that the chief cashier in London is accessing the system from a terminal in Paris, that is immediate cause for concern and something most system managers would question. Of equal concern, though, should be the person who is logging in from the next door office, or the next desk.

Staff, so far as possible, should be discouraged from moving between terminals. If this is fairly strictly observed, it is often possible to spot the unauthorised user who is using another user's login, but from a different terminal.

9.9 Disk and Tape Security.

9.9.1 Removable Storage Media.

In all probability you will have one of two types of removable storage media on your system: floppy disks or streamer tapes. A few micro-computer systems are now starting to arrive with removable cartridge Winchester disk drives, as well, but these are relatively new.

At the moment there are major variations in procedures for dealing with both floppy disk drives and streamer tape units.

In addition, such units are rather different from the rest of the computer system, which will either have no moving parts, being electronic, or have such moving parts in a protective environment (as with the hard disk drives) or are not particularly critical (as in the case of the keyboard). Since disk drives are mechanical, they are one of the most vulnerable parts of a computer system and the wide variety of differences in units compounds the problems this poses. At the very least, you should take the view that with disk drives the system may go wrong even if it does not appear possible! With this attitude in mind, you will be well prepared to take the appropriate actions to forestall disaster.

During its operation the actual disk surface is travelling at speeds of between 100 and 250 Kilometers per hour. The read/write head flies over the surface of the disk at a distance of between 1/50 and 1/10 of an inch above the rapidly moving surface touching the surface during read and write operations. In some disk drives the head is actually touching the disc throughout all operations. The surface of the disk is a rather soft magnetic oxide, which can easily be damaged. Even apparently minor blemishes, like a fingerprint smudge, or a smoke particle, present dangers.

If you consider the gap between the disk and the disk head to be represented by the height of an average man, a smoke particle would be as big as a two storey house. Fingerprint smudges can be represented by small office blocks and, on the same scale, dust particles and human hairs, which are not unlikely to become lodged on a disk surface or in the drive itself, become twenty storey hotels and office blocks.

A smoke particle or fingerprint on the surface of the disk is quite sufficient to cause a head crash, for data to be lost, and for the disk to be physically damaged, in extreme circumstances. With larger debris, like a human hair, you may even get physical damage to the disk head itself, resulting in the loss of the disk drive.

Another factor can be a build up of oxide from the disks on the disk head. This arises from contact between disk and disk head which causes oxide to be removed from the disk and deposited on the disk head. Such a build up of oxide inevitably impairs the efficiency of the disk head, and prevents it carrying out read and write operations properly. This can result in major losses of data. Oxide can also build up on tape streamer heads, with similar problems.

It is therefore essential to take care of both disk drives and tape streamer devices, to clean them regularly, and to take steps to ensure that any loss of data is minimised.

9.9.2 Disk and Tape Head Cleaning.

There are a number of proprietary kits on the market which provide you with the materials and instructions on how to clean the disk drives and tape streamer units. Such cleaning activities should be carried out on a regular basis, otherwise it will tend to be forgotten. On heavily used systems this should be at least once a week. Even on the most lightly used system head cleaning should be carried out once a month.

In addition to this, you should also have the whole system physically cleaned on a regular basis. This should be undertaken by specialist staff and can normally be arranged as part of your service or maintainence contract.

9.9.3 The Need for Backups.

A regular routine should be introduced to make backups of all material stored on magnetic media. The aim of backups is three fold, to provide:

- Copies of files in case the files are lost through some form of system failure.

- Copies of files in case disks containing the files are damaged or corrupted.

- Sufficient information to reconstruct the system where the system is physically destroyed, i.e. due to flood or fire.

The method for making backups will be discussed in the chapter on copying - see **dump** and **restore**, **cpio** and **tar**. Here we will look at some of the factors which must be kept in mind when dealing with back ups.

9.9.3.1 Backing up Originals.

There is a fundamental rule in computing that you should never work with an original source disk. The risks are too high that some disaster may take place and damage it. As soon as you receive your source copy of a program you should make working copies of it and store the source copy somewhere safe.

A major problem which has arisen in the micro computer world with respect to this is that many software houses have produced source disks which are 'copy protected'. That is they have some features encoded on them which prevent normal users making copies. These features have been introduced to prevent software piracy, although this is something they have failed to do for as soon as somebody comes up with a copy protection system, somebody else will find a way around it.

'Copy protection' has however meant that legitimate users have been at risk. The fact that many software houses offer to replace damaged master source disks at a nominal price is no safeguard. It can take a relatively long time to obtain a replacement disk with the result that a company will be without vital computer programs for a unacceptable period of time.

Fortunately, at the time of writing, the introduction of 'copy protected' software has not made itself felt in the Unix world. Many Unix experts consider that the production of such software for a Unix system would not be possible. This is due to the fact that it must be possible to install Unix software on the hard disk system and such a procedure requires that the floppy disk with the original program on is copyable. On the other hand, software designed to run on micro computer hard disk systems has been copy-protected. Without doubt as Unix and Unix-like systems become more popular and they spread into the broad world of micro computer users, some software houses will introduce some forms of copy protection which will make copying source programs difficult. This is more likely to be true of Unix like systems rather than true Unix system. In any case, because such procedures would restrict your control of the file system they would be totally against the Unix philosophy.

In order to safeguard your system, it is necessary to take a strong attitude towards copy-protection, if and when it becomes a threat. The basic rule must be that if you are offered any software which is copy protected, refuse it. The difficulties that it poses for a system manager are too severe to be treated lightly.

A different problem which faces all computer users is data decay on magnetic media. Any magnetic media which is stored is subject to the general flux of background electro-magnetic fields. This will cause a decay in the strength of the magnetic differentiation on the surface of the media and therefore of the quality of the data that has been stored. There is also evidence, especially with poorer quality media, that long storage can in any case result in physical deteriation of the media itself. The most common example of this is warping of the disk case, which can result in disk head crashes because the drive cannot cope with anything but a flat disk surface.

There was an approach to this problem on mainframe systems, based on the idea that it was unsafe to store information on magnetic media for more than six months. This applied not only to data but also to application programs. This attitude is probably correct and it is wise to adopt a routine that reflects it with regard to the magnetic media in use on your system.

It is usual to find instructions on software that working copies should be made and then the source disks should be put away and stored somewhere safe in case they are needed to make new working disks. Due to the danger of corruption of magnetic media, it has always been the rule on mainframes to refresh stored data at periodic intervals. A procedure should also be adopted on mini and micro systems and a routine established to ensure that any master copy of software is not more than six months old.

First, though, you have to decide how many copies you need of your software. The very minimum is three:

-One copy to work with.

-One copy to keep on hand near the computer installation in case the working copy is damaged.

-One backup copy which should be kept off site to supply a replacement in case of damage to both of the first two copies.

This is essential in case any catastrophic event, such as a fire, takes place.

If you work on this basis, with a set of three copies, the rotation procedure should be that, at the end of, say, six months, the work copy is removed from use and re-formatted. The on hand copy then becomes the work copy. The off site copy is brought back on site to become the on site backup copy. A new copy is made from this to become the off site backup copy.

It is important that if such procedures are followed the disks are clearly identified. One procedure which can be very useful is to colour code the labels on disks (or nowadays even use coloured disk covers) and ensure that at any one time only one colour coded disk type is in use. This will ensure that the correct copy is in use at any one time and that somebody has not failed to undertake the appropriate rotation.

9.9.4 Storage of Floppy Disks.

As they are so prone to damage, floppy disks must be stored carefully.

The first rule is that whenever they are not in the computer they should be in their sleeves. Disk sleeves, like ball-point pens, seem to have a specail ability to vanish. You are therefore always likely to be faced with the problem of a number of disks for which you do not have sleeves. Although not always possible, you will sometimes be able to purchase disk sleeves on their own. If you place a reasonably large order for disks, for example, you may be able to obtain one additional sleeve for every ten disks. It is worth trying at least. Another alternative is to make some up for yourself.

No matter what, you should never have a disk out of the computer which is out of its sleeve. If you make this a cast iron rule, you will save a lot of trouble.

A second concern with storage is how to keep floppy disks which are in use at the computer site. These should be stored in some form of covered container. There are a number of products on the market for doing this, which range from a disk file tray to vinyl covers for inclusion of disks in ring binders.

What you choose to use is very much a matter of personal choice. It is worth ensuring, however, that you make sure they are the type with dividers.

The storage of the working copies is relatively simple. When you start to deal with the on and off site backups, things become much more complicated. In theory such backups should be kept in magnetically shielded cases in properly insulated safes. Best of all they should be kept in special safes designed for the protection of magenetic data media.

Such measures tend to be fine in theory but are beyond the budget of most system managers. You may be able to persuade the board to let you spend a few thousands of pounds on the computer system, but try to obtain a small amount of money even for a filing cabinet and you have problems. Therefore we will have a look at the theory and then what is really practical.

In theory backup copies should be stored in containers which provide protection from electromagnetic interference and radio-frequency interference. They should also be stored in a container which will protect them from fire.

To deal with the latter point first: most fireproof safes and filing cabinets are designed to protect paper, but magnetic media is far more sensitive to heat than paper. There is also the problem of humidity and water. The basic way of fighting a fire is with water. When you put water onto a fire you get steam, which brings about a rise in the humidity. This protects paper from the effects of heat. Traditional fireproof safes are therefore not generally designed to protect against humidity. Humidity damages magnetic media and so ordinary fire proof safes are not very suitable.

The only real answer to the problem is to get one of the special safes designed for the storage of magnetic media. While these are both fire protective and magnetic shielded, they are also expensive.

An alternative solution, but one which carries an element of risk with it, is to make use of some of the recently developed carrying cases for magnetic data media. These have generally been designed to protect magnetic media when it is going through X-ray equipment at airports and the like, where it is not the actual X-rays which damage the media but the electro-magnetic fields which the X-ray equipment produces.

Although not so effective a protection as special safes, these containers will provide a general protection against electro- magnetic interference. The containers can then be placed inside a normal safe or filing cabinet. Although it must be realised that this proceedure does not produce a high level of security, it is a practical solution, especially if it is supported by removing a complete back up set of all data and program disks from site.

Sometimes we have the feeling that computer security people are going over the top. What they say may be relevant for the major corporations with massive security and data protection problems, but it is questionable whether such excessive measures really apply to smaller installations. For example, at one recent exhibition there was a data storage safe, which the salesman claimed was so well shielded from magnetic interference that it would protect magnetic media from an electromagnetic pulse generated by a ten megaton nuclar device detonated at a distance of ten kilometers. Unfortunately he was unable to say if it would protect the contents from the other effects of such a detonation or what the use would be of such survival to the average installation.

In contrast with the thoretical position, the practical measures that you ought to take are these:

-Keep working copies of disks stored in a covered container.

-Keep a back up copy of disks stored somewhere safe on site.

-Keep another set of backups stored off site.

If you follow these minimum precautions, you can be certain that any losses you suffer will be kept to the smallest practical levels, while at the same time you are doing all that is both cost-effective and sensible. If you establish regular cleaning and backup routines, with proper rotation of your magnetic media copies and backups, the problems you will encounter will be readily surmountable. That is the most assurance that you can gain, even if you were to make a much more massive investment. it is therefore by far the best course.

Chapter Ten

Users and User Groups.

10.1 The User.

Once the system is up and running, it is ready for the user to login and create havoc.

It has often been said that the only problem with the Unix operating system is the users: the system works fine if left on its own, but people have a habit of messing things up. This is an easy view to take of any operating system as a system manager, but particularly easy if that operating system is Unix. Part of the aim of this book, however, is to discourage this attitude, and show how being a system manager can still allow friendly co- existence with your users.

Technically a user can be a single person, or a group of people who all share the same identity as far as the system is concerned. (This point does not apply to all Unix-like systems.) Unix will allow a user to be logged on at more than one terminal. This can be a very useful facility as it can allow a number of different users to have the same user ID. It also allows a single user to use more than one terminal at once. This might sound strange, because at first sight there do not seem to be many good reasons to use more than one terminal at any one time. There are sound reasons, however. If, for example, you invoke a process from a terminal which locks that terminal up, you may want to log on as yourself from a different terminal in order to kill that process.

Some system suppliers regard this ability to log on at more than one terminal at once as a security risk. It has therefore become the practice amongst some suppliers of Unix-like systems to allow a user to login only from one terminal at a time. It can be argued, and will be later by us, that the increased risks are more than outweighed by the advantages and that with correct use, this ability to log on at more than one terminal can be turned into a security advantage.

In any case, each user is identified to the system by a User Identification Number, the UID. This number is to be found in the entries in the file **/etc/passwd** and must be unique for each user.

10.2 User Groups.

Each user on the system is also a member of at least one user group. To explain the user group concept it is first necessary to give a very brief outline of the rules governing file access. These will, of course, be dealt with in more depth later.

Each file on the system has associated with it a set of access permissions. These permissions control the type of access allowed to a file by different classes of users. The first permission in the set covers the type of access allowed to the owner of the file. The second permission in the set covers the type of access allowed to users in the same user group as the owner. The final permission covers all other users.

A user group is a number of users who share common rights and privileges with each other. This sharing usually is derived from some common interest in the use of the system. This can be illustrated by looking at an example of a small software house. This software house has the following staff structure:

-A chairman who deals only with the other members of the board.

-A managing director who is essentially responsible for product development.

-A company secretary who is responsible for the general adminstration of the company.

The above group can be defined as the management group.

Below these members of the management group, there are product development staff consisting of one programmer/analyst and two programmers who work under the direct supervision of the managing director. There is also a sales manager who has to have a high level of contact with software development.

Here we have a group which can be defined as product development.

Parallel to these is the administration staff, which consists of an account clerk, a secretary and two clerical assistants. The sales manager works with this group as well.

This gives us a final group structure that is illustrated in Figure 2.

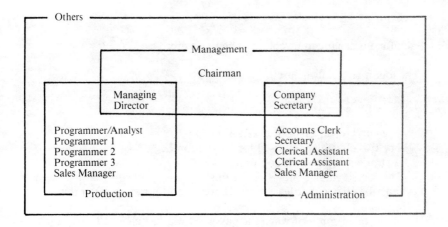

Figure 2

An interesting point to notice about this structure is that two members of the management group overlap with other groups. This means that they will have two group memberships: their primary membership of the management group and their secondary group membership of either production or administration. The sales manager, however, does not have an overlap. This is because the functions in production do not relate to administration or vice versa. There are, in fact, two different user identities on the system, one for the sales manager as a member of the production group and one as a member of the administration.

On any system there is of course certain material which is of interest to everybody using the system. The simplest illustration of this is the command structure in Unix. For this reason Unix type systems recognise a group which consists of every person registered on the system. This is the group known as: **others**.

10.3 Adding Users to the System.

Information about users is kept in the file **/etc/passwd**. This file consists of a series of entries. Each entry consists of seven fields. A typical entry is given below.

```
bob:drxRP3hxxjOL.,90/A:11:3:Sales Manager 78678:/usr/sb:/bin/rsh
```

Each field is separated by colons. The fields are:

-The logon name of the user.

-The password field, consisting of:

  -The encrypted password drxRP3hxxjO
  -The two character salt used for encryption L.
  -A subfield divider, the comma
  -The forced change provision: in this case the 90 means that the password must be changed at least every 11 weeks and no more often than every 0 weeks.
  -an encoded count of when the password was last changed, /A, which is in weeks since the beginning of 1970.

  (There can be a number of variations in the exact structure of the password field depending on the system in use. Not all systems support the forced changing of passwords.)

-The numerical user identification.

-The group identification number.

-This field in not used by Unix, and it is generally used by the system manager to store administrative information, in this case the position and internal telephone number of the user. On certain Unix-like systems this field is used by the system.

-The path to the user's home directory.

-The user's login shell. If this is left blank the default login shell will be used. This is generally **/bin/sh.**

Before you can add a user to the system you have to give them a user name, generally called the login name. This name is used by the system for the purpose of identifying the user at login. It therefore needs to be unique. If you have a only a few users, you can check the login names quite easily by listing the file /etc/**passwd** with **cat** or by using one of the editors such as **vi**. Unfortunately if you are on a large system this is not so easy and here you would be better advised to make use of one of the standard Unix utilities **grep**.

If you wish to add a user to the system with the login name **nigel,** we need to search the file /etc/**passwd** for any entries beginning with the word nigel. This can be done using the command line:

```
$ grep '^nigel' /etc/passwd.
```

The ^ at the start of the expression to be searched for indicates to the shell that this word must occur at the start of the line. Should any lines be printed then the name is not unique and you will have to find another name.

On many Unix and Unix-like systems you will find utilities which enable you to add new users. Many versions however still require you to add new users by directly editing the password file.

To edit the file /etc/**passwd** you must be a superuser.

The first stage before you do anything else is to make copies of the files which you are going to have to alter in order to add the new user.That is /etc/**passwd** and /etc/**group**. As both these files are in the directory /etc it makes sense to change to that directory first.

Before going through the procedure for making the backup copies on the system, a note about 'operational backup files'. This is the term applied to copies of files upon which work is being carried out in order to be able to restore the file to its original condition if mistakes are made. There is a convention that these files should be given a suffix which makes them immediately recognisable as backup files. Unfortunately there appears to be no generally accepted standard as to which suffix should be used.

People coming to Unix from micro systems generally tend to use the suffix .bac to indicate that a file is a backup copy. This is a personal preference, having become accustomed to it through its general usage by word processors on CP/M and MSDOS systems for backup files. The problem with this is that on certain mainframe and mini-systems, .bac is used as an extension to indicate a BASIC file. How they have arrived at that usage is something of a mystery as the general usage on micros of .bas for BASIC would seem more logical. Another variation which carries some logic is to add the suffix .old to the file name.

In practice it does not matter what suffix you use so long as you are consistent about it. It is important, however, that you, as system manager, make sure that any naming conventions you set down are kept to by all users on the system.

The command sequence to follow in making backup files is :

```
$ cd /etc

$ cp passwd passwd.bac


$ cp group group.bac
```

If you don't like the extension .bac to signify a backup file you can use your own. We will however assume that you have used .bac for the purpose of this chapter.

The above procedure will create two new files in the directory /etc, named **group.bac** and **passwd.bac**.

A further reminder is not out of place, that you should always remember to make backup copies of any file on which you are going to work, before starting to use one of the editors. This is especially important when you are dealing with system files like /etc/passwd.

The next stage is to use one of the editors to amend the contents of the password file. In this example we will be using the editor **ed** as this is commonly found on Unix systems, although you may prefer to use a different editor.

One word of warning: make sure you know how to use the editor in question before you start editing system files! If you are not certain, take the opportunity to read one of the standard introductory books to Unix and have a good practice with the editor you have chosen to use, before you start working live.

Assuming that we are using **ed**, it needs to be invoked. The following is the command to invoke ed and the file we need to edit:

```
$ ed passwd

686

*
```

There is no need to give the full path name as with the file **passwd**, as we are already in the directory /etc. **ed** responds by displaying a number on the screen, which is the number of words in the file. This is followed by the display of the command prompt *. What we need now is a display of the last line in the file. This can be obtained with print command in **ed: p**.

```
* p
```

```
rici:dav89!BHvatLP,41/a:53:5:/usr/sales/rici:
```

This is the last entry in the file. We need to add our new entry after this, and can do this using the append command within **ed: a**.

We can now make our new entry. The first field is the user name, so here we will enter **nigel** followed by a colon.

Next we come to the password field. The password is encoded by the system, so cannot be entered at this time. The password section is therefore left blank. The last part of the password field is the frequency change section. This is the part which follows the comma.

An important note here is that not all systems support this facility and you should check with your system documentation first before entering anything in this section.

Here we are concerned with the mechanics of creating forced password changes. Following the comma are two characters which have numeric values attached to them. The first character represents the number of weeks which can go by before the password has to be changed, the second character the minimum period allowed between changes. It is possible to set this minimum period to zero, but this is not advised as it would allow users to change passwords and then immediately change them back.

There is one problem here in that the characters may be numbers but they do not represent themselves. A table of the numeric equivalents of the characters is given below:-

Character	Numeric Value
.	0
/	1
0	2
1	3
2	4
3	5
4	6
5	7
6	8
7	9
8	10
9	11
A	12
B	13
...	...
Y	36
Z	37
a	38
b	39
...	...
y	62
z	63

If, therefore, you want to make somebody change their password every twelve weeks and not more frequently than once every four weeks we would enter in the password field

```
:,A2:
```

Please note that with forced changes there are two special conditions recognised by the system with regard to the values given in the field. The first is where you do not want the user to be able to change the password. In this case you enter a set of values where the first value is less than the second value. The most normal way to do this is to enter ./. This results in the values being 0 and 1. The other special condition is where you wish to force a user to change his or her password on login, but not have a set forced change thereafter. This is achieved by entering .. in the force change section. The result of this is that upon login for the first time the user will be forced to change his or her password, and as he or she does not have one yet this will mean selecting a password. After this the system will remove the periods and the user will never again be required to change his or her password by the system.

In this particular case, we want the user to change the password as soon as he or she logs on for the first time. So we will enter ,.. in the password field followed by a colon.

We now come to the user **id** number. This again must be unique.

The last user **id** used was 53 and the easiest way to ensure that **ids** are unique is to always add one to the last **id** used. Sometimes, however, you may wish to use a user's **id** which has already been used, but where the user has been removed from the system. This is particularly appropriate when you wish to allow a new user to take over files which have been the property of a previous user. In such a case you only need to give the new user the same **id** as the previous one.

To contradict what was said above about the user id having to be unique, some Unix type systems actually enforce this, but most do not and will allow you to give two users the same ID. In general practice this is undesirable, which is why we put the information in the order we did. There can, however, be a few cases where it is useful. To show this, we must see what happens when the user shares an **id**. Internally the system recognises the user by the **id**. When it needs a user's name it will look this up in the password file, starting at the beginning of the file and working through it until it finds a match for the **id**. Therefore if two users have the same **id**, after logon the system will recognise them both as being the first user with that **id** in the /**etc/passwd** file.

One way this can be useful is in the area of security and the user **root**. Most systems insist that there is a user in the file /**etc/passwd** called **root**. This is the name of the superuser. Unfortunately this does present a weakness in security. For most normal logins, an unauthorised user has to find both a login name and a password which are valid. As he or she knows there is a user named root on the system, it is only necessary to find the password. One way round this is to make **root** a no login user (see section on denying access later in this chapter) and have another user later in the login file with the user **id** and group **id** of 0. A problem with this approach, though, is that it also disables the **su** command, as this will look for the password in the **root** entry.

Fortunately there is another answer. It is becoming increasingly the practice to build systems which allow you to use other names for the superuser than **root**. On systems where you have access to the source code for login, it is also possible to amend the login procedure so that it will not accept **root** as a login name.

This means that you have to login with another name.

In our case we want a unique user identification number. We will add 1 to 53, and enter 54, again followed by a colon.

The next field is the group identification number. Here you must enter the **gid** (group identification number) of a user group. In this case we will give the same user group as for rici, that is 5.

The next field is not used by standard Unix systems, but is used by some Unix-like systems. Here some care has to be taken. Check your system documentation and find out if this field is used. If it is, make the appropriate entry. If it is not, as in standard Unix, it can be used for keeping administrative information. A fairly standard practice is to keep a note of the user's full name or position and internal telephone number. In practice you can put anything you like into this field so long as you remember to end it with a colon.

The last but one field is the path name to the user's home directory. It is normal practice to give each user a directory with the login name as the directory name. These directories are normally either in **/usr** or a subdirectory of it. In this case we will give nigel a directory in **/usr/sales** so the entry in this field will be **/usr/sales/nigel** followed by the obligatory colon.

Finally, the last field, which contains the path name of the shell that user should enter upon login. If it is left blank, as in the case of rici, the default shell, **/bin/sh**, is used. In this case this is acceptable for the entry, so the field is left blank.

Having made all the above entries, we can now press **<return>**.

Then, in **ed**, we enter a period on the next line to quit the amend mode.

The whole procedure on screen looks like this:

```
a

    nigel:,..:54:5:Sales Director 6787:/usr/sales/nigel:

    .


    *
```

If you want to check that you have made the correct entry, which is always a good idea, you can do so using the **p** command within **ed**. Then issue the **w** command to write the file to disk. Make sure that you do this before quitting.

The next step is to quit editing **/etc/passwd**. To do this you type the command **q** which returns you to the shell.

It is worth restating that the above example has been carried out using the editor **ed**, and in practice you can use whatever editor you are most familar with. We have used **ed** in the examples only because it is fairly standard on all Unix and Unix- like systems.

Check that the new user has been added to the file **/etc/passwd** by using the *cat* command to display the file.

    $ cat passwd

There is no need to give the full path name of **/etc/passwd** as you are in the directory **/etc**.

Having confirmed that our new entry is the last one in the file, we have to add nigel as a user to the user group which has the **id** asigned in the password file. You should already know the name of this group. If you do not, you can find it by using the **grep** command in the form **grep 5 /etc/group**. This will list all the lines containing 5. For our illustration we will assume that the **gid 5** belongs to a group called **sales**. If you have not already made a backup copy of the file **/etc/group** you should make one at this point.

Here again the procedure is to edit the file containing the information about the groups, **/etc/group**. Using **ed** this can be achieved with the use of the append and print commands. The procedures are as follows:

    $ ed group

    126

    * /sales/

    sales::5:tony,rici,mike

    * s/=/,nigel/p

    sa.es::5:tony,rici,mike,nigel

    * wq

First of all above, we invoked **ed** then used the search command within it to find the line containing sales. This is the command line **/sales/**. Next using **s/=/,nigel/p** we appended the user name to the end of the line. Note the inclusion of the comma before the name. If this is missed out you will have problems. Finally the commands were given to write the file and quit the edit mode **wq**.

We have now completed the processes of adding a new user to the /etc/passwd and /etc/group files. That, however, is just the beginning of the complete process. For the user to be able to login he or she must have a home directory to login to. We have already decided that he or she will have one particular directory in the password file. To complete this action we need to alter the parent directory to that proposed new directory. First we must change our working directory to the parent directory we have selected for the user's home directory, in this case /usr/sales. To do this we use the **cd** command.

```
$ cd /usr/sales
```

We are now in the position to create (or make) the new directory, using the normal directory make function of **mkdir**. In this example, we will give the directory the name **nigel**. It is general practice to give the home directory the same name as the user's login name. This is only for convenience, but it can save you a great deal of time. Should you need to look at a user's home directory, for example to amend the **.profile** file, you will not need to go first to the /etc/passwd file to find out which directory it is. The fact that you know the user's login name gives you the name of the home directory.

Directories, of course, have owners and groups. The directory is owned by the person who created it. In this case the creator was the system manager, who is a superuser. This, however, will be the home directory of the user who has just been added. You need, therefore, to change the ownership of the directory using the command **chown**. You will also need to change the group attributes of the directory to match those of the new user. This is done with the command **chgrp**.

The whole procedure for making a new user's home directory in the parent directory /usr/sales is:-

```
cd usrsales

mkdir nigel

chown nigel nigel

chgrp sss nigel
```

To check everything you can now use the command **ls -ld nigel** which will give you full details of the directory.

10.4 Profiles and User Profiles.

When a user logs into the system, the login process looks at the system file **/etc/profile**.

This file contains a series of statements which set up system variables and carry out specified processes.

An example of an **/etc/profile** file could be:

```
stty erase "^h" cr0
TERM = vt100
export TERM
umask 022
PATH = .:bin:usr/bin:$HOME
export PATH
trap cat /usr/local/logoff; echo "" 0
```

The **/etc/profile** file sets variables for the whole system.

The requirements of specific users may be very different from the general set up as given in the **/etc/profile** file. A classic example of this is the case of **root**. With most users it is advisable to start a search for a command from the current directory. For security reasons this is not advisable with **root**, so the PATH for **root** should not start with a period which means current directory.

Special requirements can be set for individual users by placing in their home directory a **.profile** file. This will be read by the login process during logon.

A typical **.profile** file could look like this:

```
PATH=.:/bin:/usr/bin:/usr/sbin:/usr/sss/nig/sbin
TERM=PC
export PATH TERM
stty erase ''^h'' quit ''^y''
echo Hello Nigel, your login time is 'date'.
echo There are at present 'who | wc -l' terminals on
line.
trap '$HOME/.logout' 0
```

The first line of this file sets up a path for the system to search for a given command. In this case the search will start in the current directory, then proceed through /**bin** and /**usr**/**bin** to the subsequent directories given in the list. Individual directories within the path are separated by a colon.

The next line defines the terminal type for this user as being PC. This is a name given in the file **termcap** for a specific type of terminal. Information is given in this file about the characteristics of the terminal. This will be read and the system set up according to those characteristics.

The user may use certain special keys for specific functions, which have not been set in the **termcap** file. The command line **stty** sets these special functions. In this case erase will be set to ^h and quit will be set to ^y.

The two echo lines print messages to the screen and provide information as the to the date and time of login and the number of users on the system. This is done using the standard Unix commands of **date** and **who**, the last one being piped through **wc** using the -l option.

Some Unix shells, like the C shell, carry out a logout procedure automatically. The standard shells on Unix, like the Bourne shell and most shells on Unix-like systems, do not do this. The final line traps the logoff signal and carries out the instructions given in the file **.logout** in the user's home directory, before logging off. This is a way of implementing a standard logoff procedure from within shells which do not have that function automatically.

10.5 umask

If you look back a couple of pages at the example of the file /**etc**/**profile**, you will see in it an entry **umask 022**. It is probably best to discuss this here, though it might be argued that it could come under security.

Whenever a user creates a file or a directory, it is assigned a set of access permissions. These permissions are assigned according to the value of the variable **umask**.

When a user logs onto the system the **umask** variable for that user is set to the value that is given in the file /**etc**/**profile**. The standard value given to **umask** in /**etc**/**profile** is 022. With this as a default value, users will have read, write and execute rights to their own files. Members of the group to which the owner belongs will have read and execute rights too, as will all others.

Although this is fine for most cases, such general access rights are not suitable for all users. For instance, it is a common practice for **root** to have access rights set automatically for the files that belong to root, so only root has read, write and execute rights on them. This is generally done for safety. Where it is desired to place an alternative setting for **umask** this can be done by making a **umask** entry with a different value in the **.profile** file of the user.

The value of **umask** is an octal value which is calculated from the binary form of the permission. To calculate this value, first list the desired permissions in a symbolic form, with **r** for read, **w** for write and **x** for execute. For the standard permissions this would appear as follows:-

user			*group*			*other*		
r	w	x	r ,	−	x	r	−	x

Then convert this symbolic notation into binary form:

user			*group*			*other*		
r	w	x	r	−	x	r	−	x
1	1	1	1	0	1	1	0	1

The next step is to write down the binary compliment of the above by changing all the ones to zero and all the zeros to one.

user			*group*			*other*		
r	w	x	r	−	x	r	−	x
1	1	1	1	0	1	1	0	1
0	0	0	0	1	0	0	1	0

To finish off you need to write down the octal equivalent of the complemented binary value.

user			*group*			*other*		
r	w	x	r	−	x	r	−	x
1	1	1	1	0	1	1	0	1
0	0	0	0	1	0	0	1	0
0			2			2		

This might justly seem a rather complicated process. It is, but things are made easier by using one of the set tables which gives you the modes. A copy of such a table is given below. It is important that you understand how such mode settings are arrived at. If, in the future, you start to delve into the actual workings of the system, you will find that it provides you with a clear insight into what is going on.

10.5.1 Table of umask Mode Setting:

	READ	WRITE	EXECUTE
0	Y	Y	Y
1	Y	Y	N
2	Y	N	Y
3	Y	N	N
4	N	Y	Y
5	N	Y	N
6	N	N	Y
7	N	N	N

10.6 Deleting Users from the System.

There are times when, especially after a user has crashed the whole system for the third time in one week with an illegal command, you may want to remove a user from the system. Our personal recommendation would be slightly more extreme than mere deletion! But deletion is highly effective for getting rid of the user. It does however leave you with the problem of what to do with the entry in the password file and the files that belong to that user.

The user's files can be a major problem for a number of reasons. The simplest reason is that they take up disk space which may be needed by other users. There is also a security problem which can arise if a user has confidential information in files and those files remain on the system after the user has been removed. Should a new user be added to the system who has the same user **id** as the one who has been deleted, then any files on the system which were owned by the deleted user will be considered by the system to be the property of the new user.

Another factor which needs to be kept in mind is that some files which a user may have, may be used by other users on the system and may be needed on the system after the user has been removed from the system.

The first thing which you need to do is get a list of all the users. This can be done making use of the **find** command, with the option **-user** and the action **-print**. As a user can have files anywhere on the system and not necessarily in the user's own directory tree, the search with **find** should be started at /. (See the section on the **find** command for more details of this.)

As there are likely to be a number of files on the system for any user, it is advisable to direct the output of the command into a file from which it can be read. The format which can be used is:

```
find / -user [user name] -print > [filename]
```

It should be noticed here that the **find** command is being used by the superuser **root**. This is essential as the search must be conducted through all the directories on the system. If you did it as a normal user you might find yourself locked out of certain directories.

Once you have the list of files belonging to the user, you can then proceed to examine the files and take appropriate action. This will normally be to archive and then remove them. Note that no file should be removed from the system until it has been archived. There is always the chance that it may be needed later.

You may want to change the ownership of some files and move them to other directories. Others you may want to leave where they are but change the ownership of both the directories and files to that of the new user who is going to be taking over.

Once you have carried out the process above, you can edit the files **/etc/passwd** and **/etc/group** to remove the user from those files. Please note that it is important that you do not remove the user until you have finished removing all the user's files from the system. It is quite a good idea before undertaking the final removal of the user to run the **find** command once more just to make sure you have not missed anything.

It is probably worth giving a further word of caution here. Many sources recommend using **find** with the **-exec** command to deal automatically with a user's files. The most common procedure is to change the ownership to whoever is taking over. Although this type of procedure is quick and easy, we do not recommend it for the following reasons:

-It is very rare that all the files a user has will have to be dealt with in the same way.

-Even if you are absolutely certain that all a user's files have to be treated in a specific way, there is always the chance that there might be something on the system you are unaware of. It is therefore advisable to check each file specifically.

-Going through the above procedure forces the system manager to think about the structure of the system, and this is nearly always a good idea.

10.6.1 Denying Access to a User.

Of course getting rid of a user completely is not always a good idea. Sometimes you just want to keep a user off the system for a period of time.

The reason why you wish to deny access to a user is fairly unimportant. He or she may not have paid the bill for computer time used, or may be hogging the computer excessively to play Wumpus, while you are trying to print out the end of year accounts. More importantly, he or she may have abused the system and you want to make your point. Whatever the reason or reasons, given that you want keep somebody off the system there are a number of ways in which you can go about it.

First you can just change the user name in the file **/etc/passwd**. This has the effect of removing them from the system. When they try to log on the system will search through the **/etc/passwd** file to try and find the user and when they are not found, will deny them access.

Another method, one much more favoured, is to edit the password field for the user in the file **/etc/passwd** and replace the entry with an invalid entry. It has become fairly standard practice to use the entry ***NO LOGIN***.

The major advantage to this approach is that when the file is listed you can see immediately which users have had access denied to them by this method.

Another word of warning might be proper at this point. One system manager thought he would make life easy and just change the user name of any user to whom he was denying access to **NOLOGIN**. The users quickly learned of this and started logging in as **NOLOGIN**. This is not an option open to them if the alteration of the password is used.

The problem with both of the above methods is that the user will get a message saying that theirs is an incorrect login. This will often result in a user thinking he or she has forgotten the password or that there is a fault in the system. This can result in a great deal of time answering questions from locked out users.

One way round this is a more complicated method, but one which we would normally recommend. Here you set up, as the program to run on login for the user, one which will print a message on screen then immediately log off the system. This approach has the advantage that the user is informed that he or she is being kept off the system.

10.7 Adding User Groups to the System.

From time to time you will have to add new user groups to the system. This is done by editing the file /etc/group. For our example we will use the editor **ed**. The layout of the fields in the file /etc/group is:

-Group name:
-Group password:
-Group **id**:
-List of login names of group members.

The first field is the group name. As with the user name, this should be unique within the list of group names.

The second field is the group password. This is left blank and is generally not used. Most system administrators and system managers advise against the use of group passwords due to the number of difficulties such usage can produce. The feeling against group passwords is so strong that many versions of Unix and Unix-like systems do not support the command for writing the password to file. But even though this field is not in use the system still expects it to be there and you have to provide an empty field.

The third field is the group **id** number. Here, as with user **ids**, the best way is to add one onto the number of the last group **id** used.

This is then followed by a list of names of the members of the group, each name separated by a comma.

To add a group called **salman,** with two members, **phil** and **tony,** to the system, the procedure is as follows:

```
cd /etc

cp group group.bac

ed group

187

* p

accnt::19:paul,steve,jenny,lin

* a

salman::20:phil,tony

.

* w

* q
```

If we follow this through in order, the first command invokes the editor, **ed**. This is followed by the information from the editor which tells us how many words there are in the file. We obtain a print of the last line in the file with **p** and then use the command **a**, within **ed**, to add the line **salman::20:phil,tony**. The period on the next line takes us out of append mode. We then give the commands to write the file and to quit the editor.

10.8 Restoring Passwords.

Sooner or later you will be faced with the sight of a rather lost user standing miserably in front of you, informing you that they have forgotten their password. This is not such a disaster as it might appear.

There are, however, a number of things to be kept in mind. First do not tell the user off for forgetting the password. Make light of it. It's not important, and you can quickly correct the situation. It is important that the user is made to feel that this is the type of thing which is expected from time to time and one of the reasons that you are there, to help when this happens.

If you don't take this attitude, but instead get upset, you will be creating problems for yourself. The last thing that you want is a situation where users start to worry about the possibility of forgetting their passwords. In such a situation they will start to write the passwords down. This is a threat to system security and will in the long run present you with far more problems than you are faced with in having to do a few password restorations.

The first thing you should do is actually establish that the user has forgotten the password. Often a user will come to you stating that they have forgotten their password, or have got it wrong, when the incorrect login message is being produced by other causes. Amongst the possible causes are:

-You have denied them access to the system by altering the user name or the password.

-There is some fault of the keyboard or input system on the user's terminal and although the user is entering the password correctly the information is getting corrupted on its way to the system. The easiest way to check this is to attempt login from another terminal.

-Somebody has planted a Trojan Horse program in your system to imitate the login routine and collect passwords. This is more difficult to check on. One way however is to execute **login** from within normal user mode, that is enter the system as one user (not the superuser), then execute **login** to change to another user. This will involve you in having to enter the password for the user. If it is found to be correct, then you may have a Trojan Horse program on your system, see the chapter on security.

If finally it is found that the user has forgotten their password you will need to restore this by logging on as a superuser, then invoking the **passwd** utility to change the password for the user.

Note that there is no way you can easily find out what the original password was. But since there is a good chance that this can have been compromised, it is best to change it.

The steps which have to be taken therefore are:

-Login as the superuser.

-Invoke the **passwd** command giving the user's name as the argument.

-Enter the new password.

-Confirm the new password.

There are really no problems in carrying out this process. The problems when the superuser has forgotten his or her password are more severe!

What you need to do is get into superuser mode, then remove the password entry from the password field in the file /etc/passwd. You then go to multiuser mode, login as the superuser, who now has no password and invoke the command **passwd** to enter the new password. Here, of course, there is a danger in the fact that for a limited period of time, albeit very short, the status of superuser is not password protected. You should therefore ensure that no other user has access to the system whilst you are carrying out this process.

The big problem is how to obtain the required status to edit the file /etc/passwd. There are a number of possible means, and the one you use will depend on the configuration of your system and the type of users you have on it.

If you have a system with privileged users, these may be able to edit the file /etc/passwd. If this is the case then login as one of these, or get them to login for you and carry out the edit.

If you have a system with more than one user name carrying the identity of the superuser, then see if you can login as the second superuser name.

If you have a system which comes up in single user mode, carry out the edit whilst in this mode.

If your system comes up automatically in multi user mode and you cannot bring it up in single user mode, then you have to **IPL** from an alternative boot device in single user mode.

If none of the above are possible then you will have to get Unix reinstalled.

A major word of warning. There are some system managers around who keep a file on their system which will automatically set the password for **root** to null. These are designed to be used in an emergency and can be executed by any user on the system. Such shell scripts, for most of them are just shell scripts, are a major threat to the system security. We would advise that they are never installed on a system. The theory behind them is that they are hidden in a mass of files and unless the user knows the name of the script they cannot invoke it. This is a mistake. It is common practice, not to say routine, for unauthorised users to try out any command they don't know.

If you do feel that for your peace of mind you have to have such a shell script available, then don't keep it on the main system files. Keep it on a floppy disk, by itself, and keep that disk locked safely away. In this case, if you do forget your password you can restore the situation by mounting the disk and then executing the shell script.

A problem with this is that it would require the **mount** command to be executable by an ordinary user. This is not generally a desirable situation. One way around this is to write a special shell script to carry out the mounting and execution of the file.

As a general piece of advice, however, we are opposed to the use of such files.

Chapter Eleven

The file System under UNIX.

The sheer power and flexibility of the Unix file system is one element that has ensured its success as an operating system. Since it is so powerful and flexible, inevitably it is complex, and this is one of the main problems.

In theory, too, it is possible to have a Unix or Unix like system with just one file system on it.In practice, however, any Unix or Unix-like system is likely to contain a number of different file systems.

There are two main aspects of the file system that concern us here. The first is the physical structure of the file system. That is the way in which files are laid out on the disk and how you can access them. The second is the logical structure or form of the file system. This is really the nature of files, the structure of directories and everything else at this level.

We will deal with the latter questions first, and then come to the physical aspects of the file system. This is partly because the physical aspects are, in general, less relevant to most system managers, and partly because the next chapter, which deals with the command **fsck** naturally leads on from a discussion of the physical aspects of the file system.

Essentially, the Unix or Unix-like system has a file structure which can be described as hierarchical and dynamic, with structureless files. What this really means is that each directory is related to other directories on the file system and is either above the one you are relating it to, as a parent directory, or below it, as a daughter directory. In practice the relationship is often much more complex than that, but this will become clearer as the file system is explained. Secondly, the files are said to be dynamic because they can be changed in size at will. They are also said to be structureless, because the way in which a file is made up is more or less dependent upon the program that produces it.

These three terms, hierarchic file system, dynamic files and structureless files will be explained in more detail here.

11.1 The Hierarchic Structure.

Unix was one of the first operating systems on small computers to offer an hierarchical file structure. This means that directories can contain directories, which in turn can contain directories. There are two main advantages to this type of structure. It allows for a logical structuring of the storage of related files, since all the files related to sales, for example, can be held in a directory callled **sales,** while each salesperson's files can be held in a directory inside the sales directory. By the same token, all the files related to accounts can be held in a directory called **accounts,** with each customer having a separate directory held in that parent directory.

Such an approach leads to a far more effective operational use of a system, in that there is no need to search through a mass of unrelated files in order to find the few related ones you need. Since they can all be held in the same directory, subdivided if necessary into further directories, the task of grouping files is relatively simple. This approach also helps to build in a certain amount of security. If all related files are in the same directory, access to sensitive information can be limited by restricting access to any directories you want kept from general view.

In practice, of course, things become a good deal more complex, and not altogether so effective. Yet the Unix system does attempt to provide these facilities.

One consideration that will become more important to you when running a system is access speed. An hierarchical directory structure improves access speed considerably and takes up fewer system resources. The average time taken to access a file inside a hierarchical file system is a good deal less than the time taken in a sequential file system.

In order to achieve the best results from using a hierarchical file system it is necessary to be very careful about the way that it is structured. If, for example, you merely begin to place a large number of files within a directory, without much concern for their relationship with each other, or their relationship with parent or daughter directories, you will to all intents and purposes be creating a sequential file system out of a hierarchical file system. This will result in a substantial loss of performance if not checked.

Another distortion that can enter a file system is the over- production of directories. Some users get into the habit of opening a new directory every time they want to open a new file. In little time, it is possible to arrive at a file system which looks like the structure in Figure 3 below:

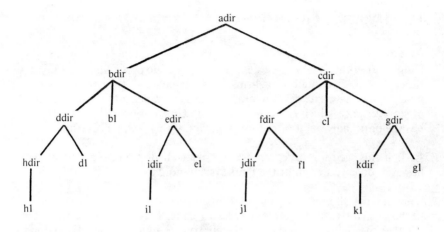

Figure 3

In this case, which is by no means extreme, we have ten files and 11 directories! This makes no sense in most commercial systems and produces a real overhead in absorbing system resources.

Not only do human users acquire this sort of habit, but some application software takes a similar approach. It is not unusual, for example, to find an application which opens a new directory for every new document, and a new file for every new page in that document.

Such applications are, in general, badly designed and a very poor investment. As system manager you have a responsibility to check all software before it is implemented or installed on your system. One solution is to refuse to run such applications until they have been modified to take a more sensible approach to system resources.

That is not to say that there are never any occasions when a new directory for a single document is inappropriate. They are extremely rare and need to be justified each time. However, there can be a case for it where, for example, you have a large number of restricted users running application software on a system. Here each user might well have a home directory which contains only one file, which is of particular concern to the application that needs to be run.

In general, though, be very careful about adding new directories indiscriminately.

11.2 Dynamic File Structure.

Unlike most other operating systems Unix applies no preset limits to the size of files. They are free to grow or shrink as the demands of the system require. In practice, files have a tendency to grow. What can happen is that you will run out of storage space, which is the only limit that Unix imposes. If you do so, Unix has the unfriendly habit of not warning you of this fact, and crashing.

At first this seems a rather strange approach. It does make a type of sense, however, once you examine the Unix system more closely.

Unix handles all input and output through files. All devices, like printers and keyboards, for example, are only files to Unix. It is of no concern to Unix whether the file is actual data or merely your terminal display. Everything is treated like a file.

While there are clearly limits to the size of data storage devices, there are no such limits to device files. To place any form of limitation on file size would, in practice, put restrictions on keyboards, which would mean that effective use of devices would be limited.

The answer is vigilance. The system manager must always check the system to ensure that there are sufficient resources to meet the demands that are being placed on it during any operational session.

If you follow a regular routine of system maintenance, there should be no problem.

11.2.1 Flexible File Structure.

Unix, unlike other operating systems, does not impose any pre-ordained structure on files in its file system. In fact, it only recognises one type of file: a sequential series of bytes of information. Any specific format within the file, and means of accessing parts of such data as may be present are determined by the software program and not by Unix.

This means that your files may be sequential data files, random access files or indexed files. The choice is entirely with you, or the programmers who write the software.

11.3 Forms of Files.

11.3.1 Ordinary files.

Ordinary files consist of a sequential series of bytes which many contain one or more "gaps". Ordinary files are dealt with by the operating system by using the system calls: **seek**, **read** and **write**.

"Gaps" in files occur during writing to files. If the file pointer, for example, is positioned past the end of the file by the **iseek** system call, a **write** command is given and a "gap" will appear in the file. Where this "gap" covers complete blocks, these will be unallocated and will remain in the free block list. Where such a "gap" occupies a part of a block, it will show as null characters.

11.3.2 Special files.

Special files are Unix files which refer to devices, like the terminal display or a printer.

11.3.3 Directory files.

Directory files contain a list of filenames within a directory, together with the inode number connected with those particular filenames. They provide the operating system with a means of locating the address of a file through the **i-list**, when the name of the file is given.

Directory files are flagged as such by the operating system and the access permissions are different from ordinary and special files.

11.4 Physical Layout of the File System.

A file system is laid out on a logical disk. It starts at block zero and continues to the end block on the disk. There is a file system on every logical disk on the system with the exception of the swap area, which contains a special configuration.

It needs to be noted here that the figures in the following part of this chapter refer to a Version 7 Unix compatible system. They may not apply strictly to your system. The sequence of parts will, however, remain the same. The main difference is that on systems using a block size of more than 512, it is standard practice to place the boot block and superblock in one physical block.

The first disk block of the file system is numbered 0. This is the boot block. On all file systems, with the exception of the root file system, the boot block is not used.

Block number 1 on the file system is the superblock. In many ways this is the most important block on the system, because if it is corrupted beyond repair, there is little chance of saving the data on the system.

The superblock contains data about the file system, its name, the location of the top of the **i-list** and the location of the free block list.

The structure of the superblock is as follows:

1.   The number of blocks in the **i-list** (this includes the blocks 0 and 1).

2.   The number of block on the system.

3.   The number of addresses in the array which contains the first free blocks.

4.   An array containing a list of the first free blocks on the system.

5.   The number of inodes in the list of free inodes.

6.   An array containing a list of the first free inodes in the **i-list**.

7.   A flag used to lock records during free list manipulation.

8.   A flag used to lock records during **i-list** manipulation.

9.   A flag used to indicate that the superblock has been modified.

10.   A flag used to indicate that the file system has been mounted in read-only mode.

11.   Time of last superblock update.

12.   Total number of free blocks.

13.   Total number of free inodes.

14.   The interleave factor used on the system.

15.   The interleave cylinder size.

16.   File system name.

17.   File system pack name.

Items 1 to 11 are generally maintained on all Unix and Unix like systems. There can, however, be quite a variation in items 12 to 17. Details of precisely what is on your system can normally be found in the file **/sys/filsys.h**. The problem is that highly cryptic names tend to be used, as is common with the C language environment. A translation of the standard names is given below. Note that not all systems have kept to the following standard, though it is in general use, with minor variations.

s__size   The number of blocks to the end of the **i- list**. That means, in practice, the number of the highest block in the **i-list**.

s__fsize   The number of blocks in the whole file system.

s__nfree   The actual number of block numbers in the array **s-free**.

s__free [**NICFREE**] An array with the first free blocks.

s__ninode The actual number of inodes in the array **s__inode**.

s__inode [**NICINODE**] An array with the first free inodes.

s__flock   A lock flag used during manipulation of the free blocks.

s__ilock   A lock flag used during manipulation of the free **i-nodes**.

s__fmod   A lock flag used to indicate that the superblock has been modified.

s__ronly   A flag used to indicate that the system has been mounted in read only mode.

s__time   The time that the superblock was last updated.

s__tfree   The total number of free blocks on the system.

s__tinode The total number of free inodes on the system.

s__m   The system interleave factor.

s__n   The system interleave cylinder factor.

s__fname   The file system name.

s__fpack   The file system pack name.

Once a file system has been mounted the image of the superblock for that file system is kept in memory. This is the reason why flags are used to indicate that parts of the file system are, or have been, modified.

11.4.1 The i-list.

Immediately after the superblock is the start of the i-list. This continues upward to the block given in the system variable, **s__isize**.

The **i-list** contains a list of inodes. In each inode, information is contained about the file system and the files on it. The copy of the inodes held by the system in memory while a file system is mounted contain additional information which is not held in the disk version of the inode. The information held in the disk version of the inode is as follows:

1. The access mode of the file and the type of file.

2. The number of links to the file.

3. The owner's user identification.

4. The owner's group indentification.

5. The number of bytes in the file.

6. A list of the first 13 disk blocks of the file.

7. The time the file was last accessed.

8. The time the file was last modified.

9. The time the inode was last modified.

Full details of the structure of the inodes can be found in the file **/sys/ino.h**.

The names used for the variables are

di__mode   Protection data and type of file.

di__link   Number of links to the file.

di_uid	Owner's **uid**.
di_gid	Owner's **gid**.
di_ize	Number of bytes in a file.
di_addr	List of first 13 bytes.
di_atime	Last time of access to file.
di_mtime	Last time of change to file.
di_ctime	Last time of change to inode.

In addition to the information above, the **incore** copies of the i- nodes contain a reference count, a device identification and an inode number. In some versions, the reference count is also kept in the disk copy.

The role of the inode is important. In directories the only information held with respect to a file is the file name and the inode number of that file. When the system finds the file it is searching for in a directory, it reads the inode number and then reads that inode. From this it can find the location of the first ten blocks in the file. These are directly addressed through the inode.

Block 11 referred to in the inode is the indirect block. This is a block which contains the addresses of the next 128 blocks, if they are claimed. Blocks 12 and 13 refer to blocks which themselves refer to more data blocks. This gives double and treble indirect addressing, respectively.

The figures above refer to the operation with block sizes of 512 bytes. In theory, on this basis, you could address, through one inode, up to one gigabyte. In practice, on most systems, you would run out of space well before you did so! If you are running a system with a few gigabytes of store, you will probably not be interested in Unix.

11.4.2 Allocation of inodes.

The superblock contains an array which lists the first of the free inodes. Free inodes are marked in **i-list** by having **di_mode** set to the value 0. When an inode is required, the system takes the number of the inode from the bottom of the array, and all entries above it drop by 1. When an inode is freed, for example when a file is removed from the system, the **di__mode** in that inode is set to 0, and the number of that i-node is placed on the bottom of the array. The array therefore operates as a last-in-first-out (lifo) stack.

If the array is full, the number of the free inode is not placed on the stack. Should the array become empty, the **i-list** is scanned , starting with inode number 1 and working up, to locate inodes with the **di__mode** set to 0. These are then placed in the array until the array is full. If there are no inodes found free, an error message will be given and the system will crash.

During the scanning of the **i__list** the flag, **s__ilock** is set. This flag prevents other processes which need free inodes from proceeding until the array has been filled.

11.4.3 The Free List.

The free list is a list of all the blocks which have not been allocated as data blocks, and are therefore not being used for files.

A list of free blocks is kept in the array **s__free** in the superblock. This cannot, of course, hold all the free blocks in the file system. If, however, it does, it means that you have problems because you are running out of space.

The remaining free blocks are listed through a series of secondary address lists. The first entry in the free list is a number giving the number of free blocks in the array. Immediately after this is the number of a block, which contains another array made up in the same way. In this fashion, the first block number in each array gives the address of the next array holding lists of free blocks.

This chain structure can be seen in the Figure 4.

11.4.4 Data blocks.

Data blocks are blocks in the file system which are claimed by the inodes for holding data. The positions of such blocks is recorded in the inodes themselves, or through the indirect addressing system associated with the inodes.

Data blocks, free blocks and the free list are interleaved on the file system.

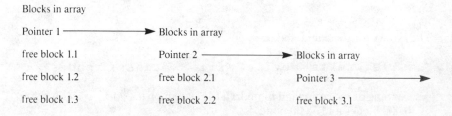

Figure 4   *Pointer chain structure for free list.*

11.4.5 Overall Structure.

The overall structure of the file system may therefore be throught of as laid out in Figure 5.

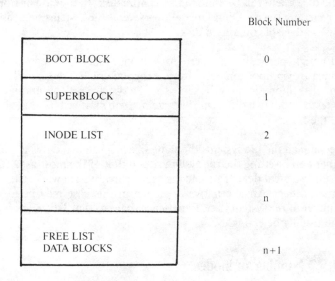

Figure 5   *Overall Structure of file system by block distribution.*

11.5 Making a File System.

The Unix command for making a file system is **mkfs**, which is located in the directory **/etc**.

The syntax for the command is:

```
/etc/mkfs <device> <size> <number of nodes>
```

An example of the command to make a file system on disk device 3 with a size of 10,000 blocks and 3,000 nodes is:

```
$ /etc/mkfs /dev/dsk3 10000 3000
```

Stating the number of nodes is, however, optional, and where it is omitted the system will supply the default number of nodes. This is arrived at by dividing the number of blocks by a given number, which is generally 4, but on some Unix-like systems the number can be 8.

11.5.1 File System Size.

The file system can be as large as an entire disk. In the case of floppy disks this is generally the case, but Unix allows several file systems on a single disk, and this is advisable on a hard disk.

Although particular file systems will inevitably be used more heavily and increase disproportionately in size, it is good practice to keep all the file systems on a disk approximately the same size.If a system crash occurs and it is necessary to restore files to a different file system, there may well be insufficient space for all the files.

Keeping all the file systems the same size helps to avoid this possibility. On the other hand, setting the file system size to that of the most used file system will result in a great deal of wasted disk space on a system where use of file systems varies widely. An alternative approach in this case may be to use a limited number of file system sizes. Experience suggests that 3 different file system sizes will usually be enough.

11.5.2 Number of inodes.

Every file on the system requires one inode. The default number of inodes is the number of blocks divided by 4, although on some systems this can be 8. Using the standard number 4, a system with 10,000 blocks will give 2,500 inodes and a possible 2,500 files. Although this sounds reasonable there are potential problems.

Bearing in mind that Unix System V uses 1 kbyte blocks, it is clear that the best average file size is four kbytes. If, however, all your files are only two kbytes, your system will run out of inodes while only half the blocks are used. In this way, half the disk space is wasted. At a different extreme, if all the files are 50 kbytes in size, you will run out of blocks while some 2,000 inodes are still available. Indeed, there will be space for less than 200 files, since some blocks will be taken by the unused i-list. In this way, unnecessary inodes will take up valuable file space.

In order to establish the optimum number of inodes for your system, you have to have a good idea of the average file size. By converting this to blocks and dividing it into the total number of blocks on the system you will have a good idea of how many inodes are required. If the average file size is large, however, it is good practice to allow an extra number of inodes for safety.

This will be clearer by taking an example of the problem and the particular solution reached. A specialist publishing company has a 10,000 block system, divided into three separate file systems.

The first file system is used for correspondence, most of which is short, perhaps a page or even less in length. Most files are therefore under one kbyte, although some might be four kbytes. The average file length is therefore one block. If this file system occupied the whole 10,000 block, it would suggest that 10,000 inodes would be required, dividing the total number of blocks by the average file size.

The second file system is used to store texts. These are between 20 and 30 kbytes in length, very occasionally reaching 40 kbytes. The average file size is 28 kbytes, making 28 blocks. By using the same method as before, about 350 inodes seem called for. In practice, however, a relatively small decrease in the average file size would result in many wasted blocks. It was decided to increase the number of nodes to 400 to allow for such a possibility.

The third file system is a more difficult case, since it is used for customer accounts. A large number of files are kept, which vary widely in size from one kbyte, for overdue account reminders to over 500 kbytes for the main customer database. The average file size is approximately five kbytes, which shows that there is a high proportion of small files. The standard method of dividing the number of blocks used by each file into the number of blocks available would indicate that some 2,000 inodes would be required. The high proportion of small files, however, means that it is safer to accept the default number of inodes, 2,500, giving margin for safety.

Only experience will really enable the system manager to determine what is the optimum number of inodes for any particular system. The default calculation, dividing the number of blocks by four or sometimes eight, will provide a good base from which to start.

Chapter Twelve
find and ls.

12.1 The find Command.

The **find** command is used to find files which meet specified conditions. It can also be used to carry out certain operations on the files which have been found. The selective use of this command gives the system manager a very powerful tool.

The syntax of the command is:

```
find [pathname-list] [condition-list] [action- list]
```

The **find** command usually starts its search in the directory indicated in the pathname-list. It will then search every specified directory and subdirectory to discover which files meet the conditions identified in the condition-list.

This means that if you want to search more than one directory, it is only necessary to list the directories you want searched, putting a space between each directory name. Not all versions of **find**, however, support this facility of having more than one start directory and you will have to check whether your version does.

There is a tendency to start all searches from the root directory, which means that every file mounted on the system will be examined. This is bad practice, not least because it takes far longer than a much more careful use of the command.

Under the root directory, /, you will have a minimum of four subdirectories, and most Unix-type systems will require many more than four. The first two in most cases will contain the system files, and there are very many of them! If you give the root directory as your starting point for a **find** command, each of these is going to be examined needlessly, since you will very rarely be interested in your system files.

It needs to be stressed that the **find** command is very demanding in terms of system time and resources and needs to be used with care. Using **find** indiscriminately will very often result in many complaints from users about deterioration in your system's performance.

One point worth considering from this viewpoint is whether you can use **find** in background mode or not. If your use of the **find** command will result in alterations being made to files, you are advised to work in interactive mode, using the option **-ok**, detailed below. If, however, you are absolutely certain what the results will be, you can still use the command in the background.

Using **find** in background mode is obviously advantageous, particularly if it can be given a low priority. If this is possible, judicious use of the **nice** command to reduce its priority as much as possible will make the least noticeable demands on the system. This will make a difference to other users of the system, particularly if you cannot run the command when other users are not very active.

In any case, it is much better to be selective about the directories you are going to subject to a **find** command. The ability to be this selective will rely on having a good, working knowledge of the tree structure on your system, and knowing where you should start when using a **find** command will save you a great deal of time, and release a significant part of your system's resources.

As a general rule, however, you will probably be safe starting a **find** command from the **/usr** directory, which will usually contain the files you will be interested in within its subdirectories.

There are a number of conditions which you can specify when you are using the **find** command. These are:

```
-name [filename]
```

This condition will identify all instances of the file or files which have the the filename specified. This can be very useful, particularly with the use of the wildcard, *, which is provided by the shell. For example, if you know that a particular user always adds the extension .ngi to his or her files, you can search for that user's files with the command:

```
$ find /usr -name *.ngi

-perm [onum]
```

This condition will find all examples of files which have the octal permission mode **onum**.

```
-type [x]
```

This will find all instances of files specified by x. x may be:

d directory files

f ordinary files

c character device files

b block device files

p named pipe

   `-user [user-name]`

This will find all files which have the owner specified by user- name. The user **id** can be substituted for the user-name.

   `-group [group-name]`

This will find files which belong to the specified group. The group **id** can also be substituted for the group-name.

   `-size [n]`

This will find all files which are n blocks in size. Where -n is specified, the command will find those files which have less than n blocks, and where +n is specified, files containing more than n blocks will be identified.

   `-links [n]`

This will identify those files which have n number of links to them. If -n is written, **find** will identify those files which have less than n links, and more than n links where +n is written.

   `-atime [n]`

This will find those files which were accessed n days ago. Just as above, -n will identify files which were accessed fewer than n days ago, while +n will find those files which were accessed more than n days ago.

   `-mtime [n]`

This will identify any files modified n days ago, with -n showing files modifed more recently than n days ago, and +n showing those files modified more than n days ago.

```
-ctime [n]
```

This condition will identify those files changed n days ago, and -n and +n can also be used.

These conditions can be made more powerful by using them in conjunction with logical operators. Details of these are given next.

Any conditions placed together within brackets will be operated on first. The shell, unfortunately, gives a special interpretation to brackets, so it is necessary to protect bracket signs and show the shell that they are really brackets, by placing a backslash in front of them each time. This means that you have to write a pair of brackets in the following way: \ (and \ ), thus escaping the usual treatment given to brackets.

Conditions can be given the reverse or a negative meaning by preceding them with a NOT operator: !.

They can also be linked by a logical **and** by placing the conditions on the same line.

A logical **or** can be invoked by using the -o option between conditions and enclosing the conditions you want treated this way inside brackets. It is necessary to use the backslash, of course, as in this example:

```
$ find \ ( -type d -o -user enid\ )
```

This command will find all files which are directory files, or which belong to the user enid.

Once the **find** command has found files which meet the specified conditions, a number of actions can take place. These are specified in the action-list.

In Unix-type systems there are four action-list options, which are:

```
-print
```

This will display the pathname for the files which meet the condition-list criteria.

```
-exec [command]
```

This, the most powerful of the action-list options, will execute the specified Unix command. This command can be any of the Unix commands without restriction.

```
-ok [command]
```

This action-list option works just like the -exec option, but you will be asked for confirmation before the Unix command is carried out. This is especially useful where the Unix command may make a permanent alteration to the file or files specified, as in the case of **rm**. It has the drawback, however, that you cannot use **find** in background mode.

```
-cpio [device]
```

This will make copies to the device specified of the files which meet the criteria in the condition-list. This can be used, for example, for archiving your security backups. (See the section on **cpio** for more details.)

find is therefore a very powerful and useful command for the system manager, particularly when dealing with the routine jobs so often associated with this role. For instance if you needed to remove the user nigel from the system, you will probably also want to remove all his files as well, once they have been backed up. This could be achieved using the command line:

```
$ find /usr -user nigel -cpio /dev/rk1 -ok rm
```

12.2 The ls Command.

Every Unix user will probably claim to be familiar with the **ls** command, so why is it necessary to discuss it here? The simple answer is that most users are not really familiar with it. All they know is the basic command.

The **ls** command has a number of options which can make it very useful both to a normal user and a system manager. We do not have space to cover them all, and there is some variation between implementations, but notes are given below on some of the most useful options for the system manager.

The one option which most users are familiar with is the - l option which gives a long listing, as shown here:

```
= ls -l


total 283

drwxrwxrwx 2 root system    120 May 5 09:48 Admin
-rwxr-x--- 1 root system   9873 Apr 9 14:28 Ltaal
-rwxrwxr-x 1 phil system  12876 May 6 12:38 Ltaal#
-rwxrwx--- 1 phil system 121908 May 3 21:19 Prolib
```

In this listing the figure at the top refers to the total number of disk blocks
occupied by the files listed. In the actual listing, the first column gives you the
type of file, whether it is a directory file or otherwise, and the access
permissions. The next column tells you the number of links to the file. this is
followed by the owner's name and the group that owns the file. Next we have the
number of characters in the file, then the time and date the file was last written
to. Finally the name of the file itself.

It is often necessary for the system manager to know which files in a directory
are active, that is, being used, and which are not. This is especially true when you
examine a file system with the view to removing files in order to generate disk
space. Often, especially if you have a hogger on your system, you will find that
there are a number of files which are obviously just updates of each other, but
it might not be clear which is the current version in use and which are the older
versions.

If the -t option is used in conjunction with the **ls** command the files will be listed
in order of modification time, with the latest modified being listed first.
Sometimes, however, you may not be interested in when a file was modified,
only when it was last accessed. In this case you will need to use the **-u** option.
This can be very useful in finding out if a file is still in use. For instance, if you
have a help file on the system and you may want to find out if people are still
using it. If the file is called **/usr/train/help**, for instance, you could check if it is
used, with the command:

```
$ ls -lu /usr/train/help
```

This would give a single line in long listing format but with the access time
replacing the modification time. If the file has been accessed recently then the
facility is obviously still being used, but if the last access was some months ago
then it is fairly safe to say it is not being used and may be removed from the
system.

Another option which is quite useful is the **-c** option which lists the last modification time of the inode in the order they occurred. This is important if you are checking things like changes in file permissions, which cause alterations to the inodes, but no change to the file itself. One illustration of where this might be used is when you know that there has been an unauthorised access to the system and suspect that some file access permissions have been altered.

The -r option enables you to reverse the order of the sort, which is very useful if you are *piping* the output to another command. If you want to know the number of blocks that are being used by a file then use the -s option.

The options given above are generally the same on most Unix and Unix-like systems. There are other options available, in particular some specialised ones which are system specific. You should read your system documentation and try out the various options to see what the results are, because **ls** is a very powerful command which can help you in many ways, but the real power of **ls** becomes available to you only when the options are combined and the output *piped* to other commands.

Chapter Thirteen

Backup and Archives.

Although the terms, *backup* and *archive*, are often used loosely as though they mean the same, there is a distinction to be made between them, which is helpful. Here we use the two terms to mean separate activities and we think it is important to preserve that distinction.

A backup copy, therefore, is a copy of a file, file system or part of a file system, which is intended to be used to restore the material that has been copied should the original be damaged in any way. The essential thing about a backup copy is that it is intended to provide a back up, hence its name.

An archive copy, on the other hand, is a copy of a file, file system or part of a file system, which is intended to provide a version of the original as it stood on a particular date. Archive copies are not taken with the primary intention of being able to restore the original, but so that you can go back and use it as a precise record.

In some cases making a distinction between the two types of copy may be academic, but it is always useful to be aware that a distinction does exist. It still leaves the question open, however, of why you need to make backups and archive copies.

There are a number of reasons why archive copies can be important. For example, certain auditing procedures may require that records can be checked in the exact form they were on a specific day. There are security factors as well. It is sometimes useful to check a file which you suspect may have been illegally amended against a copy which you know has not been.

An interesting illustration of the latter point was a case of a multi-user system, not Unix, which had a large number of users who were connected to the system by the public telephone network. Shortly after being appointed, following the retirement of the previous system manager, the new system manager started to get evidence that there was an illegal user on the system, but could not trace how the user was getting in.

The user file, the equivalent of the the Unix password file, contained over six hundred authorised users. There was also an archive copy of the user file taken immediately after the last amendment to it. Upon examining the current user file against the archive copy, with a program that compared the two automatically, it was found that the file had been amended. A user who had been deleted from the system by having the login flag set to no access - the method on this system for deleting a user - had been reactivated. The illegal user was then using this as the identity under which to log in. Once this was established it was possible to set a trap to catch the illegal user.

Not all cases of using archive copies are as interesting, but archive copies are still important. Take the case of a user who cannot remember if a specific procedure has or has not been run. If that procedure updates files, this can be checked by comparing one of the files which the procedure should have updated against an archive copy of that file.

The reasons for making backups are similar, of course, to making archive copies. The first reason is the possibility of having the misfortune of a disk crash. These might be increasingly rare, but they still happen. You might be lucky and find only part of the file system has been destroyed, but you will still need backups to recover what is missing.

A second reason, and far more common, is where the file system has been corrupted. This usually occurs as a result of an improper shut down of the system.

The third and most likely reason for needing a backup copy is when the user accidentally erases a file or a file system. This, as we all know full well, should not happen with well trained users. Unfortunately such paragons of computer virtue are not that common. Even system managers have been known to erase the wrong files.

There are a number of questions to be answered by the system manager with respect to archiving and backup. The first is which method of creating a backup or archive copy should be used, since most Unix and Unix-like systems provide a number of options, all of which have advantages and disadvantages.

The second question only needs answering if you are making a backup and that is when to carry them out. By their nature, archive copies are taken whenever certain conditions are met. For instance, if a file is to be removed from the system then an archive copy should be made. If a major change in the format of records is to be carried out, then archive copies should be made. In that sense, archive copies are always triggered by an event. Backup copies, however, are made according to a schedule.

What you, as the system manager, have to decide is how often they should be made. Here you have to strike a balance. If they are made too frequently you will find that the majority of system resources are employed most of the time making backups. On the other hand if backups are not made frequently enough, the file system will have undergone such changes as to make the backup copy worthless.

The third issue is the physical aspect of the backup, that is how the backup should be made and stored. Do you work with removable Winchester cartridges, masses of floppy disks, or with streamer tape? All have their advantages and disadvantages.

The issues are fairly diverse, and need a section on their own.

13.1 Backup Media.

One of the major problems when it comes to backup is the time which is taken to carry out such an operation. The main reason for this is the relatively slow rate at which data can be written to floppy disk or streamer tape. This problem has to an extent been overcome by the latest Winchester disks, with interchangable disk cartridges. They do provide a means of storing a high volume of data together with a very rapid transfer time.

Removable Winchester disk catridges suffer from the disadvantage that they tend to be fairly bulky. They are also quite expensive, with each one costing as much as a normal Winchester disk, which is essentially what they are. At present they have not come into general use as backup media. It is doubtful if they will come into such use in the foreseeable future.

An area where they may be of use though is in installations where intermediate level backups (see section on frequency) have to be made and where it is essential that as little system time as possible is taken up. In these sort of circumstances the high cost of the cartridges may be more than offset by the savings in system down time while the backup is made.

There is another factor which comes into consideration here and that is the compatility of these cartridges with other systems. Not many commercial institutions can afford to have two full systems on hand, one to act as a backup system if the first goes down. It is however essential for many users to have backup computing facilities. This is particularly the case with commercial concerns like building societies, finance houses and stockbrokers.

One way in which they often tackle this problem is to use computer systems which are compatible with those being used by other firms in the same location, with whom they have a mutual arrangement. The arrangement basically gives each access to the other's computer equipment, in case of emergency, so that they can continue to carry out vital data processing.

As yet, there is no generally accepted standard for Winchester cartridges and if you have such a facility on your system it is very unlikely that other computer systems locally, even from the same manufacturer, will have the same cartridges, or even accept Winchester cartridges.

This physical incompatibility is overcome to a certain extent by floppy disks. There are some fairly well defined and accepted standards for these products: 8 inch, 5.25 inch, 3.5 inch and 3 inch. Here the incompatibility problem is usually brought about by the format of the disk. Such problems can often be circumvented by using software which allows systems to read disks which are not in the format of the original system.

The main disadvantages of floppy disks is the slow data transfer rate compared with Winchester disks and their limited storage size. As your main data storage is almost certainly on a hard disk, you will probably find that its size is considerably higher than the size of any floppy disk you can put on the system. This will therefore result in you having to use a great number of floppy disks to undertake a backup.

This problem is becoming easier to solve now with the advent of floppy disk drives which have a very large storage capacity. The use of such devices coupled with limiting the size of file systems, can make backing up much easier. It can, for example, enable one complete file system on the main disk to be backed up to one floppy. This approach does however limit the size of your file systems to a level which in most commercial applications will be unacceptable. It is to be hoped that things will become easier with the development in the next few years of new floppy disk drives, having very large capacity storage.

Streamer tape and tape cartridges hold what up to now has been the main way for making backup copies. They suffer from a slow data transfer speed, but do offer large storage volume.

What is probably the most acceptable way of taking a backup at present is to use a combination of both disk and tape to make your backup and archive copies. This sort of arrangement is being used increasingly.

13.2 How Often to Take Backups.

This question of how often to take backup copies is where the system manager must perform a balancing act between competing interests. If you take backups too frequently you will have a large proportion of system resources tied up making backups.

On most systems such a situation is not acceptable, though there will of course always be exceptions.

At the other end of the scale, if you allow too great a period between backups, you will find that the value of the backup has become virtually nil, as there will have been too many changes in the file system.

Against this, however, is the fact that making a backup absorbs both time and system resources. One way to reduce this is to keep the number of times a complete backup is made to the minimum level which is compatible with successful recovery, and to support the complete backup with partial backups which only deal with the files which have been changed since the last complete back-up was done.

There is, of course, a complication with this sort of approach in that if you need to restore a file system, you first have to use the most recent total backup, then add on all the partial backups which have been made. A further awkward situation can occur when it is a question of restoring an individual file which has been lost. Here you have the problem of not knowing which of the backup copies has the most recent version of the file on it. You will have to search all of them. This is done by starting with the most recent backup and working your way through the previous ones until you find the latest updated version of the file.

Partial backups have been made easier to a certain extent with the introduction in Unix of 'dump levels'. These enable you to do backups, or more strictly 'dumps', at different levels. The concept is fairly simple. Unfortunately this is only available with the **dump** utility, and backup utilities which are based on **dump**. Fortunately it is possible with other backup and archiving utilities to make use of other commands like **find** to give the same effect as if the backup command had 'dump' levels.

The concept behind 'dump' levels, or incremental backups, will be explained in the section on **dumnp**.

A factor which must also be taken into consideration is that an increasing number of application programs are now incorporating their own backup procedures, so that backup copies of the appropriate files are made whenever the program is run. This is very useful and can often form the easiest source for restoring lost files. It should not however be relied on. You should presume when working out your backup schedule that application programs do not make any form of backup provision.

13.3 Backup Methods.

Unix provides a number of different methods of making backup and archive copies. Each has advantages and disadvantages.

13.3.1 Dump and Restore.

This pair of utilities provides a convenient way of copying an entire file system from a system disk to backup media and then restoring it. The file system is written from the system disk using the command **dump**. It can be recovered with the related command **restor**.

dump does not offer the flexibility which is provided by some other backup utilities. It does, however, provide you with the facilities to carry out *incremental backups* without having to resort to external commands. This is achieved by having a number of dump levels.

There are ten dump levels, numbered 0 to 9. At level 0, a total dump is carried out of the whole file system. When a dump is made at any other level the effect of that dump depends on the level of the previous dump. If the previous dump was at level 0, or at a level higher than that of the current dump, then all files changed since the last level 0 dump will be copied. If the dump is carried out at the same level as the previous dump or at a higher level, then only those files changed since the last dump at the same level will be copied.

To make this clear, it needs illustrating. Thus, if we start by carrying out a level 0 dump, then the whole file system is copied. To restore the system now, we have to use the level 0 tape.

If we now make a dump at level 6, it will dump all files which have been changed since the level 0 dump. To restore the system we will have to use both tapes.

If a further dump is then made at level 7, only those files changed since the level 6 dump will be copied. Now to restore the system we will have to use three tapes.

However, if instead of carrying out our last copy at level 7 we did it at level 5, then all files changed since the level 0 dump would be dumped. This means that we now only have to use two tapes to obtain a complete restoration.

This principle is often used in setting up backup procedural structures. A fairly simple structure is to make a level 0 dump at the end of each working week. During the next week, at the end of each working day, you make a dump, starting on Monday with a level 4 dump, then decreasing the level of dump by one each day. On Tuesday, therefore, you do a level 3, Wednesday level 2 and on Thursday level 1. This of course means that by Friday you are back to the level 0 dump, a complete dump of the file system. This was where you started.

The point of such a structured approach is that at any time you only need to access two dumps to restore the complete file system. The problem with this is that the amount of material dumped each day grows, so the dumps get slower and slower. This may not be too much of a problem in many commercial situations. Normally a high proportion of the files on such a system is fairly static, such as the command and program files. The highly dynamic files will be restricted mainly to application program data files. Even here many files will only be subject to changes at the end of fairly regularly defined periods.

A useful point here is that taking a backup can be made easier by selecting application programs which minimise the need for copying large data files. A simple example of this is a software package maintaining customers' names and addresses. If all changes are written directly to the main file when they take place, then every time a change takes place the whole file will have to be backed up. If the changes are written to an amendment file, and the main file is only updated periodically, only the amendment file needs to be backed up regularly. This can save considerable time and resources in backing up data files. It is of course important in these circumstances to make sure that full dumps are taken after the main data files have been updated.

An alternative method is to make dumps each day at the same level as the day before. In this case only those files which have been changed during the day will be dumped. This considerably reduces the volume of dumping that has to be done each day, saving both time and system resources. It does, however, present the problem that if you have to undertake a restoration a large number of tapes will be involved.

There are a number of possible combinations and variations on the above sequences. For instance, it would be possible to have an alternating day sequence, where you start with a level 0 dump, then make a dump at level 5, and the next day you also make a level 5 dump On the third day, however, you carry out a level 4 dump. This would mean that from then on the two level 5 dumps are redundant. The following day a level 5 dump will be done, coming round to the final level 0 dump at the end of the fifth working day.

Which approach you adopt will depend very much on your system and the requirements you have for backup copies. You may find that it is very rare for you to have to restore files, but that the time taken to do dumps causes problems for system usage. In such circumstances doing all dumps at the same level makes sense. If, on the other hand, you have to carry out a lot of restoration, then keeping the number of tapes needed to restore files to a minimum makes sense.

It should not be thought that you have to use the same mannner of making backups for the whole of the system. There is no reason why, on file systems which are relatively little amended, you should not use the method which dumps the same level each day. On another part of the system, where you have a file system which changes frequently, use one of the other methods.

13.3.1.1 The Syntax for dump and restor.

The syntax for **dump** is:

```
dump [dump level] [option] [filesystem]
```

We have discussed dump levels above. The options on **dump** are **f**, **s**, **u** and **d**.

The **u** option causes the level and date of the dump to be recorded in the file /etc/ddate. If you **dump** to streamer or cartridge tape and the length or density is not that which is set in the default for **dump** (for which you must see your system documentation), then these must be set with **s** and **d**.

s is used to set the length, which is expressed in feet, given after the option.

d is used to set the density. This value is given in bits per inch (BPI) after the option. If you wish to dump to a device other than the default device, this must be indicated by use of the **f** option and the name of the device.

For instance:

```
$ dump 0f /dev/cart0  /dev/wdisc2
```

This will carry out a dump of all file systems on /dev/wdisc2 to the cartridge tape /dev/cart0.

An important point to note is that when you are dumping from a file system to storage media which has a smaller capacity, you will have to exchange the backup media during the dump process. Most versions of **dump**, on Unix and Unix-like systems, allow this, giving a message to change volumes at the appropriate point. When this happens you should change the backup media, then press <return> in order to continue.

There are versions of **dump** which do not allow for this. In such cases you can only dump to media which is of sufficient size to hold the whole of the file sytem being dumped. You should check your system documentation with reference to this point.

When it comes to restoring a complete file-system you make use of the **restor** command. For complete or partial dumps this is used with the **r** option, which indicates that the entire file system is to be copied. Should you wish just to restore a single file then the **x** option is used.

The typical command would be:

```
$ restor r /dev/wdisc2
```

This would read the information from the default device and write the system back onto **/dev/wdisc2**.

Should you not wish to use the default device then the source device can be specified using the **f** option:

```
$ restor rf /dev/cart0 /dev/wdisc2
```

This will restore the whole system from **/dev/cart0** to **/dev/wdisc2**.

Should you have partial dumps to restore, you must first restore using the full system dump, then use each of the partial dumps in the order in which they were created. Each of the partial dumps will overwrite any earlier versions of files which are on the restored system.

If it is necessary to restore one file from a dump tape, the command is used with the **x** option. The syntax for this is:

```
restor x [filename]
```

There are a couple of points to be made about this. First, the filename must be exact, that is the full name as on the dump tape. This might seem simple, but think it through carefully for a moment. If you had a file called **monthly** in a directory called **sales** which was itself mounted under the directory **usr** the full pathname on the system would be **/usr/sales/monthly**. The first part of this pathname refers to a directory on the root file system. The **/sales** directory, is in fact a head directory for the file system containing **/monthly**. Therefore on the dump tape the name of the file will not be **/usr/sales/monthly** but **/sales/monthly**. This can be very important at times.

One way in which you can make sure that you get the names right is to use the utility **dumpdir**. This lists the names of files actually dumped onto a particular tape. Unfortunately it is not available on all systems.

The second point is that you may not get the file back where you expect it to be. **restor x** will write the file into a file in your current directory. This could of course cause problems if **restor** wrote the file back with its original name, as you might already have a file of that name in the directory. The way round this is that **restor** gives the newly written file a numeric name, which is in fact its inode number. It is then up to you to rename it and put it in the correct directory.

Care must be taken when using **restor** as it does not always carry out a correct updating of the free block list. This can be remedied by carrying out an **fsck** command after restoration.

13.3.2 Using tar.

Unlike **dump** and **restor** the utility **tar** does not allow you to make dumps at different levels. It also uses far more system resources and time. Its main advantage is that it knows about the hierarchical directory structure and files are restored to the system with their orginal pathnames. This can be very useful when moving software around between systems. For this reason it is quite normal to find vendor software supplied to you in **tar** format.

Note that although **tar** stands for tape archiver, and that throughout this description we will be talking in terms of tape, it can be used equally well with floppy disks. In fact the majority of **tar** use on smaller commercial systems these days is with floppy disks.

The syntax for **tar** is:

```
tar [argument] [option] [filename(s)]
```

There are five arguments available for use with **tar**:

```
- c
```

This creates a new backup tape. Any existing files will be overwritten.

```
- u
```

With this option an update of an existing backup is made. Any of the named files are added to the backup media if they have been modified since the backup was written, or if they are new.

- r

This causes **tar** to read the tape until the end-of- file is found and then append the named files.

- x

This extracts the named files from backup tape. If the named file is a directory, then the subdirectories and files of that directory are extracted. If no name is given then all the files on the backup tape are extracted. Any missing directories are created in the destination file system in order to maintain the relationship of the files within the file system hierarchy. If there are any files which have the same names, then these will be overwritten. This means that the last entry of a file on the tape will overwrite previous entries which are on the destination file system.

- t

This gives the names of the files held on the backup tape.

We can now move to the options, which can be used to modify the standard operation of **tar**.

- f

This allows you to specify a device other than the default device for **tar** to write to or read from. If the device name is a dash (-) then **tar** reads from the standard input and writes to its standard output. The default drive for **tar** is normally **/dev/mt1**.

- v

This provides additional information. Normally the name of each file is given as it is encountered. This can be useful, as **tar** is not a highly communicative program and many users have stopped **tar** half way through, when there has been no signs of any activity for some time and they have thought that the system had gone down. Reading file names as they come up does at least pass the time.

- m

This is used in conjunction with **x**. When a file is extracted with **tar** the modification time shown on that file is that which was present in the file when the file was read by **tar** and archived. If the **m** option is selected this will be updated when the file is extracted, to the time and date of extraction. This is most important when **tar** is being used to move files between systems.

– k

This sets the size of the media to the figure given after **k**, which is the size in kilobytes. It is important to do this when using floppy disks, or cartridge tapes which you know or suspect might be smaller than the size of the file system you are archiving.If the size of a file system is larger than the media onto which it is being copied, **tar** will split it across a number of volumes, prompting for additional volumes as needed. **tar** will also ask for additional volumes if they are needed to restore a split file system.

– b

This sets the block factor for the media. This should only be used with raw tape devices. The default is 1 (512 bytes) and the maximum is 20. This option is only used when writing to the tape, when reading the block size is automatically determined.

The above options are generally available on all versions of **tar**. There are some additional options, which are not generally available and you should consult you system documentation for details.

When it actually comes to using **tar** it is far more flexible than **dump**, though probably not quite so useful for complete file systems. With its **f** option it can be included in a pipe, taking its input from the pipe output. This makes it particularly useful in conjuction with the **find** command.

We will start with the basic level:

```
$ tar c /usr/sales
```

This creates a **tar** format tape on the default tape drive, and will copy to this all the files and directories which are contained in, and below, **/usr/sales**.

More often than not you will want to make a backup to media other than magnetic tape in the default drive. A fairly common example is to back up one set of files to floppy disk. An example which will do this, is:

```
$ tar cf /dev/fp1 /usr/sales/north
```

This will create a new **tar** format file on the floppy disk in **/dev/fp1** and copy onto it the files held in the directory **north**.

To restore a file from the disk the command is:

```
$ tar xf /dev/fp1  /usr/sales/north/june
```

An important point to remember with **tar** is that if a file is extracted with a complete pathname, then it is restored to its previous location in the file system hierarchy. It will, however, be copied into the current working directory if it is not given the full pathname. While the example above will copy the file **june** into the directory **/usr/sales/north**, if the command had been:

```
$ tar xf /dev/fp1 june
```

In this case, the file **june** will be copied into the current working directory.

Unlike when using **dump**, you cannot do incremental backups with **tar** directly. They can, however, be carried out using the **find** command. To achieve this you use **find** to search for all files which have been modified since the date of the last backup. The output of this search is used as the input into **tar**. This can either be accomplished indirectly, by writing the output of **find** into a file, or directly by piping the output of **find** into **tar**. The latter course tends to be the most popular, and where it is used a significant amount, it is often written into a shell script.

The following example will backup all the files in a directory called **/usr/sales**, which have been modified in the last two days:

```
$ find /usr/sales -mtime -2 -exec tar u {} \;
```

13.4 Using cpio.

cpio stands for copy file archive in and out. It is one of the more flexible tools available to the system manager to move files and make archive and backup copies.

As we have said before, each utility has its own advantages and disadvantages.**cpio** has flexibility on its side, but it is slow and makes very heavy demands on the CPU. It is advisable therefore that this utility should only be used at times of low system usage.

In use, **cpio** has three modes:

cpio -o This reads the standard input to obtain a list of path names, and these files are then copied onto the standard output together with path name and status information.

cpio -i This extracts files from an input, which is expected to be a **cpio** produced file. Only files which match the name or pattern specified are extracted.

cpio -p This reads the input from a **cpio** produced file to obtain a list of path names of files that are created subject to conditions and copied into the destination directory tree, subject to conditions set by certain options.

There are a number of options which are available for each mode, many of which are quite specilised in their application. You should consult your system documentation for more details. We will only cover the main options here.

To backup files with **cpio** you have to supply a list of filenames as standard input, and direct the standard output to a file or device. There are a number of ways in which the list of filenames can be supplied. You might just want to back up the files in a specific directory, in which case the output of **ls** can be piped into **cpio**:

```
$ ls | cpio -ov > /usr/sales/backup/dum
```

Here we are using the -o mode, which is the output mode. The option selected with this is **v** for verbose which causes a list of file names to be printed. If this option is used with the **t** option, which prints a table of contents, the output will look something like the **ls -l** command.

The output from **cpio** is then redirected to a file in the directory **/usr/sales/backup.**

More often, however, you will want to carry out far more complicated activities and to send the output to a device.

```
$ find / -user nig -print | cpio -oBv > /dev/cart0
```

Here we want to find all files on the system owned by the user **nig** and to archive them on the device **/dev/cart0**. This is the type of operation which would typically be carried out if you were removing a user from the sytem.

The first part of the command line is the **find** command, and the search is started from the root directory /. The condition we have selected for **find** is that of the user name, **-user**, which is here **nig**. The action selected is for **find** to print a list of all the pathnames, **-print**. The output from this is piped into **cpio**, using the output mode **-o** together with two options **v** and **B**. (The **v** option has already been discussed, above.)

The **B** option causes **cpio** to write bigger blocks than the default of 512 bytes. In the case of **cpio** this means 5,120 bytes. Unlike some other utilities, with **cpio** you cannot specify the size of the larger blocking factor.

To get the information back, you need to use the -i option:

```
$ cpio -iBv 'sales/*' < /dev/cart0
```

After the **cpio** command we get two options: **B** for bigger blocks and **v**, which is the verbose option to let us know what is going on. Next, within single inverted commas, is the pattern we want matched. This one will give all the files which have a name starting with **sales**.

The pass mode of **cpio** is used for copying parts of the file structure from one part of the system to another. If that destination happens to be on a removable storage device, then it can be used for backup. An important thing about the pass mode is that the destination directory must exist, as **cpio** will not create it.

If we are in a directory **/sales/north** and we want to make a copy of the directory to a temporary directory called **/sales/temp/north** the procedure would be:

```
$ mkdir /sales/temp/north
$ ls | cpio -pdv /sales/temp/north
```

Here the target directory, below which the structure is to be copied, is made using the command **mkdir**. After this we use the command **ls** to produce our list of file names and pipe these into **cpio** with the mode selected as pass, **-p**. The second of the two options selected is the familiar verbose option, so that we know what is going on. The first option is the **d** option. This stands for directory, and causes **cpio** to create subdirectories as required.

There are many more options available with **cpio** which give you further power and flexibility. Unfortunately this also seems to be one of the commands which suppliers like to *customise*. There is a great deal of variation within **cpio** utilities on various installations. You should carefully check the system documentation on your system to establish the full range of facilities offered.

13.4.1 The dd Command.

The Unix System V manual states that **dd** converts and copies a file. It has the ability to carry out a variety of specialist conversion functions during the copying. This makes it a very powerful and flexible command. It is also fraught with problems when you come to use it. For this reason we are only giving it a very brief mention and outlining some of the problems.

The **dd** command is used to copy between named character serial devices, or files. The two important parameters you have to remember with **dd** are **if=** to which you give the name of the input device and **df=** to which you give the name of the output device.

147

To copy from a Winchester disk known as **/dev/hd1** to a cartridge tape in **/dev/cart0** the command would be:

```
$ dd if=/dev/hd1 of=/dev/cart0
```

To restore, the parameters are reversed:

```
$ dd if=/dev/cart0 of=/dev/hd1
```

It is possible with **dd** to specify the block size using the parameter **bs=**.

Now for the problems! With **dd** the system must be quiescent. This, to a certain extent, is true with all the backup commands, but it is essential with **dd**.

Next, as the command operates solely on raw devices, it can only be used by someone who has privileged access.

There is also a problem brought about by bad blocks on the disks. Whilst the **dd** can handle bad blocks on a file-structured device, when dealing with that device in a raw serial mode, **dd** may fail on some systems. On other systems it may jump over them, but this can result in problems as well. If the information is restored to another disc, one with different bad blocks, the file pointers will now more than likely point to the wrong blocks.

It is recommended therefore that **dd** should only be used when no other utility can be in use.

13.5 File System State.

It is advisable, whatever method is being used, to keep the file system you are backing up in a quiescent state. With some utilities like **dd** this is essential. The best way to do this is to unmount the file system for the period of the backup.

Backing up the root File System.

As the **root** file system cannot be unmounted, this presents problems when it comes to carrying out a backup. These problems are compounded by the fact that should it be restored, information in memory will differ from that on disk, because of the activity going on in the system.

Should it be necessary to backup or restore the **root** file system, the best answer is to run the machine from another disk for the period of the activity. Most suppliers are able to supply a cut-down system which can be run from a floppy disk on such occasions.

Chapter Fourteen
File System Maintenance.

14.1 fsck.

As has already been explained, whenever a Unix system is started up, a check should be carried out on the file system, using the utility **fsck**. This check should also be carried out before making a back-up of the file system.

The utility **fsck**, file system check, is a program which checks the file system for consistency. It does this by making use of redundant information contained in the file system. Whenever an inconsistency is discovered, **fsck** will offer the system manager the opportuinity to repair the file system.

Inconsistencies arise in the file system because of a failure in its updating. Such updates occur whenever a file is created, removed or modified. On an average Unix system this process can take place at least many hundreds of times a day. With such a large number of processes, errors will inevitably be present, even if the error rate is very low.

The most common cause of inconsistencies in the file system is a failure to close the system down in an orderly manner. The most common cause is the failure to issue a **sync** command at this point. (See the section on starting up and closing down a system.) This omission can be due to negligence on the part of the operator, or even to a power or hardware failure forcing a premature close down.

There are, then, five types of file system updates. These relate to the superblock, the inodes, the indirect blocks, the free list and the data blocks.

14.1.1 Checks on the Superblock.

The item most frequently corrupted is the superblock, mainly because it is the most frequently used part of the structure. Every time there is a change to the file system's blocks or inodes, a modification has to be made to the superblock. The utility **fsck** is used to carry out a number of checks on the superblock to establish its consistency.

The first check is on the file system. Although there is no actual way that **fsck** can check the size of the file system, it can check that the claimed size is consistent with its use.

It can check that the file system is larger than the number of blocks used by the superblock and the i-list, and that the number of inodes is less than the maximum of 65,535. If the system is within these bounds, **fsck** will accept the size of the file system given by the superblock as valid. All subsequent checks carried out by **fsck** depend on these first checks.

The free block list, which starts in the superblock, is checked next. The first free block list is contained within the super- block and **fsck** checks that the total count given by this block is not less than zero nor more than the maximum allowed for the system.This is normally 50, though it can be higher. If it were such an impossible value, it would indicate that the super-block was corrupt.

After this check, **fsck** then checks that the blocks indicated by the free blocks list are within the data section of the file system. Once this has been done, all the block numbers in the free blocks list are compared with the allocated block list numbers. An error is reported if there are any duplications here.

If the free block list is non-zero, indicating that there are additional free block lists, **fsck** will then check these.

Once all the blocks have been accounted for, a check is made by **fsck** to ensure that the total number of free blocks claimed by the free blocks list, added to the number of blocks claimed by the inodes, is equal to the total size in blocks of the system.

The superblock also contains a count of the total number of free blocks on the system. This is compared by **fsck** with the total number of free blocks actually found in the system. If they are discovered to be inconsistent, **fsck** may replace the number held by the superblock with the actual number found in the system.

A check is carried out to ensure that the number of inodes in the system that are found to be free is equal to the number of inodes listed as free in the superblock. If they do not agree, the utility may correct the listing in the superblock.

14.1.2 Checks on the Inode.

Although inodes are individually less susceptible than the super- block to corruption, there are probably corrupted inodes, which will be listed.

The i-list is checked sequentially by **fsck**, starting with the first inode.

The inode type is checked to see whether it is a recognised type: regular, directory, special block or special character. The type of each inode is indicated by the mode word which each inode contains. If an inode does not fall into these categories, it is reported as an illegal type.

A check is also carried out on the status of each inode, to see whether it is allocated or unallocated. It if is found to be neither allocated nor unallocated, it is reported as an incorrectly formatted inode. This can happen as a result of hardware failure, when incorrect data may be written into the inode list.

Whenever an inode is of an illegal type or incorrectly formatted, the only correction available is to clear the inode.

Because each inode contains a link count, which holds the number of links claimed for the file to which the inode refers, this can be checked by **fsck**. Starting at the root directory, **fsck** checks the total directory structure, counting the number of actual links to the inode.

If the link count in the inode is not zero, but no links were found by the utility when checking the directories, it means that no directory entry has been found for the file related to that inode. It is normal in this type of case to establish a link to the special **lost+found** directory. For further details about this directory, see the relevant section.

If the link count does not match the link count recorded in the inode, and the recorded link count is not zero, a directory entry may have been added or removed without the inode being updated. In such a case, **fsck** will replace the link count in the inode with the actual value found.

Within each inode there is a list of blocks that are claimed by a file, or there are pointers to such a list. The utility **fsck** compares each block number claimed by an inode against the list of blocks that have already been allocated. If a block has already been allocated, that block's number is added to the list of duplicate blocks. If there is no duplication, that block number is added to the list of allocated blocks.

Two checks are made on the i-list to find the inodes of duplicate blocks. Without examining the contents of the files associated with the inodes, there is not enough information within the system for it to decide which of the inodes is incorrect. In practice, as a general rule, the inode with the earliest modification date is incorrect and this inode should be cleared manually.

A check is also carried out to ensure that the inode is not claiming a block outside the data area of the file system. Any such blocks are designated bad blocks.

As each inode contains a size field, this information is checked by **fsck** for inconsistencies. The main check is whether the directory sizes are multiples of 16 characters. A partial check is also carried out on file size. This is done by computing the number of blocks which should be associated with a file from the size given in the size field. This number of blocks is then compared with the actual number of blocks claimed by the inode.

14.1.3 Indirect Block Checks.

Each indirect block is owned by an inode, and any inconsistencies in the indirect block will affect the inode which owns it. The utility will check whether there is any duplication in the blocks claimed and whether there are any blocks claimed which are outside the file system.

14.1.4 Data Block Checks.

Data blocks are divided into two types: ordinary, which are sometimes called plain, and directory. No attempt is made by **fsck** to check the validity of the contents of ordinary data blocks, because there is no way that it could know what the contents of a data block should be.

As there are rules governing what directory blocks may contain, **fsck** can check these, and the check is on the inodes connected with each directory.

A directory entry inode number may be that of an unallocated inode. This can occur when something has interrupted any update, in the time between the directory entry being written and the inode being written. Such directory entries will normally be removed by **fsck**.

If the number of the directory entry inode is greater than that of the last inode in the inode list, which can occur when bad data is written into the directory block, **fsck** will also normally remove the directory entry.

Checks are then carried out on the directory inode number entries for the directories " . " and " . . ", which should be the first and second entries. The value of the directory entry " . " should be equal to the inode number of the directory data block. The value of " . . " should be equal to the inode number of the parent directory, or, in the case of the root directory, it should be equal to the inode number of the directory data block. (As **root** does not have a parent directory, it points to itself.)

If the directory inode numbers are incorrect, they can be corrected by **fsck** in certain circumstances.

A general check is made of the whole file system. If any unconnected directories are found, these will be linked into the directory **lost+found**.

14.1.5 Free List Block Check.

The free list block check checks for blocks which are outside the file system and for blocks which are already claimed by parts of the file system, as allocated blocks.

14.1.6 Running fsck.

The utility **fsck** checks the consistency of the file system against the information held within the file system. Should any changes occur to the file system while **fsck** is running, other than changes of which it is aware, errors will obviously result. It is therefore essential that no modifications to the file system take place while the utility is running.

The easiest way to ensure this is to unmount the file system before invoking **fsck**. In the case of the root file system, however, this is not possible, and it is essential that the file system is not used. This is best achieved by putting the system into single user mode.

The syntax for running **fsck** is:

```
fsck [device name]
```

Where no device is specified, the command, by default, will take the devices listed in the file **/etc/checklist**. This file contains a list of all the devices mounted during system start up. (It may be amended by using any of the standard editors.)

There are five stages to **fsck**:

-Check block and sizes.

-Check pathnames.

-Check connections.

-Check reference counts.

-Check free list.

There is also a sixth stage which involves no checking where repairs of certain types of fault can be made.

Should any inconsistencies be found, you will be asked at each stage whether any repairs should be carried out. As repairs will make irreversible modifications to the file system, care should be exercised about which repairs are authorised. Many repairs can result in lost data, for example. For this reason, it is generally advisable to reject any requests for repairs on the first run.

There are two additional reasons for this approach.

In the first place, **fsck** can show up hardware faults as file inconsistencies in certain circumstances. Should a large number of errors be revealed in a file system, especially in one which is not normally modified a great deal, hardware errors should be suspected. If repairs were to be carried out at this point, it is possible to write inconsistencies to a consistent file system. There are no absolute ways of recognising hardware errors, but experience will generally provide good indications. Guidance should also be available from your system manufacturer or system engineer. Hardware errors are, fortunately, not all that common on modern systems, and they are more generally likely to appear before being revealed by **fsck**.

The second reason for not allowing repairs to the file system on first running the utility is that data can be lost through clearing inodes. During its run, **fsck** may ask whether it should clear an inode where it has found a duplicate or bad inode. If you answer yes, a zero value will be written to that inode and any data associated with it will be lost. Such data may often, but not always, be saved using the utility for finding file names from inode numbers, **ncheck**. On some Unix-like systems, it has been modified to give the file name and not just the inode numbers, and then **ncheck** is not required in order to find the file name.

14.1.6.1 Saving data associated with duplicate or bad inodes.

We will assume that the version of **fsck** you are using does not provide file names. When you first run it, answer *no* to all the questions asking whether repairs should be carried out. When you reach the question referring to inodes is reached, it will probably look like this:

```
DUB | BAD INODE = n CLEAR Y/N
```

The exact presentation of the message obviously varies between different systems. The important part is that the inode number is given, and you should make a note of it. On most versions of **fsck** there will also be a message which gives the size of the file in blocks. If this information is present, make a note of it.

Once you have completed the first run you can attempt to make copies of any data which is likely, or liable, to be lost by clearing inodes. To do this, first of all find the name of the file associated with the particular inode in question. This can be done using the utility **ncheck**. The syntax for using this utility is:

```
/etc/ncheck -i [inodenumber] [filesystem]
```

If **ncheck** reports a file name you can then make a backup copy of the file using one of the standard Unix copy utilities. If no file name is reported, then the utility has failed to find a directory entry for that inode and making a backup is not possible.

Before making a backup, assuming that it is possible, you should first make sure that the data in the file is complete. This can be done by using the **cat** utility to read the file. Provided the data is uncorrupted, you can copy the file. Such copies should be placed on a different file system, and not the one you are working on, so that even if further things go wrong, you are no worse off than when you started!

Once you have reached this position, you can re-run **fsck**. This time you can answer *Y*, or yes, to the **CLEAR** enquiry.

14.1.7 The Phases of fsck.

14.1.7.1 Phase 1a.

Each inode is checked, then the disk blocks pointed to by that particular inode are validated. If the inode data is incorrect, the message **BAD** or **BAD INODE** will be given.

An estimate is made from the size table in the inode about the number of blocks which should be used by the file. If this does not agree with the number of blocks claimed, then a message is given, indicating a possible file size error.

If a disk block is claimed by the inode, but has already been claimed by another inode, the message **DUP** will be given.

Checks will be carried out on the size claimed for the directory files, and if these are not multipls of 16 bytes, a **DIRECTORY MISALIGNED** message will be given.

14.1.7.2 Phase 1b.

This stage is only run if any duplicate blocks are found in the first phase. It is a re-scan for duplicate blocks and will ask if they can be cleared. Answer yes to this only if you have already carried out the procedure for saving associated data.

During the first phase, you may get a message which says: **PARTIALLY ALLOCATED INODE**. You will be asked if this should be cleared. Again the answer should only be yes, if you have already carried out the procedure for saving associated data.

If during phase 1 you are given either: **POSSIBLE FILE SIZE ERROR** or **DIRECTORY MISALIGNED** as error messages, these may be corrected by **fsck** during later phases. If they are not corrected later, and re-appear on the check run, you will have to undertake a repair.

This repair should involve the following steps:

-Back up the file or directory involved.

-Remove the file or directory, using either **rm** or **rmdir** as appropriate.

-Re-run **fsck**.

-When there are no errors reported, restore the files and directories from the backup copies.

14.1.7.3 Phase 2.

The first thing which happens in this phase is that the inode for the root directory is checked. If this is found to be unallocated, it will mean that the root inode is corrupt. In such a case **fsck** will abort. In such a position, you will have to re-install Unix.

Sometimes **fsck** will find that the mode word for the root directory inode does not indicate a directory. When this happens you will get the message: **ROOT INODE NOT DIRECTORY . . .FIX?**. The answer to this should be yes. You may also get other messages telling you that there are either duplicate or bad inodes in root. These messages will ask if the utility should continue. Here, again, you should answer yes. There will, however, be a high level of risk of file system errors as a result. You may feel it is better to re-install the **root** directory.

Whether you should re-install **root** or not is something that it is difficult to give advice about. Only experience of your own system is a real guide. It is not a process, however, to be undertaken lightly!

During this second phase of **fsck** you will be given the choice of clearing the inodes found to be either duplicate or bad in the first run. Provided you have carried out the procedures outlined above, for saving the data associated with such inodes, answer yes to the questions.

There is one proviso: *it should be noted that sometimes duplicate blocks are shared between the file and free block list. When this happens do not clear the inodes. An additional phase will be carried out at the end of the running of the utility which will correct the problem.*

14.1.7.4 Phase 3.

During phase 3, **fsck** will scan the file system for directories in which the inode number is invalid. These are known as *unreferenced* directories. When they are found you will be asked whether they should be re-connected. The normal answer is yes, and this will result in a link being made between the directory in question and a special directory, known as **lost+found**. This directory is located in the root system.

It is important that there is sufficient space in the **lost+found** directory to accommodate files and directories linked to it. Refer to the chapter on the **lost+found** directory for further details about it and its use.

14.1.7.5 Phase 4.

In this phase the reference count, also known as the inode count, is checked against details collected by the utility in its earlier phases.

During phase 1 of **fsck** the reference count for each inode is set to the number of links claimed for the physical file. In each of the following two phases, this is decreased by 1, each time a valid link is found.

If everything is correct, by the time the process gets to phase 4, the reference count should be 0. Unforunately this is not always the case. If this is the case, there are two states that can exist.

The first is where no links have been found for a file. Such a file is known as an *orphan* file. You will be asked if you want the file re-connected, to which the normal response is yes. This will result in the file being connected to the **lost+found** directory. If you decide not to re-connect the file, you should answer yes to the question which will next appear: **CLEAR UNREFERENCED FILE?**

Follow this same procedure if, for any reason, reconnection to the **lost+found** directory is unsuccessful.

The alternative is that not all the links claimed by the file will have been found. Here you will be given information stating what the actual link count should be and what has been claimed by the inode. You will then be given the chance to re-adjust the count, and you should accept that opportunity.

Once the links have been established, or at least dealt with and corrected, you will be asked to clear the inodes of those unreferenced files containing duplicate or bad blocks. You should again follow the standard procedure for saving data before clearing the inodes.

A final factor which can arise at this point is a message informing you: **FREE INODE COUNT WRONG IN SUPERBLOCK**. When asked whether you want this fixed, answer yes.

14.1.7.6 Phase 5.

Finally, **fsck** will check the free block list. Should there be any bad or duplicate blocks the message **BAD FREE LIST** will be displayed. This will also be followed by the question: **SALVAGE?**. You should give the answer yes, again.

14.1.7.7 Phase 6.

If the instruction was given to salvage the free list, **fsck** will then re-construct the free list. This phase does not involve any checking of the system and may be regarded as really a repairing extension to phase 5.

14.1.7.8 Problem of Image Difference.

If the free list has been reconstructed, there is a further problem, which results from that process. The image of the file system held in memory will not match the corrected file system on disk. If a **sync** command is issued at this point, the image in memory will be written to disk, causing a recorruption of the corrected system. To avoid this happening, it is essential that the system is closed down without a **sync** command being issued.

When circumstances like this arise, you will get a message from **fsck** saying:

```
- - - - - - BOOT UNIX (NO SYNC) - - - - - -
```

What you do at this point is very dependent on your actual system. On some systems you have to switch off the power. This can cause all sorts of problems with systems which have backup power supplies. Such backup systems normally issue a **sync** command automatically on interruption of the power supply while the system is in use.

Most systems have a re-boot switch or button which will carry out a re-boot without causing a **sync** command to be issued. If you have any doubts about this on your own system, you should check the point with your system supplier.

14.1.7.9 Re-running fsck.

Should you have had any errors reported during the running of **fsck** you should always re-run it. This process should be repeated until no errors are reported. Under no circumstances should you use a file system which has shown errors under **fsck**. This can result in all errors being magnified and it will increase your chances of failing to recover the data that is at risk.

14.1.7.11 Error Messages.

In the section above we have covered the main messages which you can receive during the running of **fsck**. There are a number of other error messages which, fortunately, tend to occur rather more rarely. Short details and explanations of these appear below.

The first set of messages are likely to occur during the initialisation stages of **fsck** with each file system.

```
Can't get memory
```

fsck is unable to obtain the memory it requires for its virtual memory tables. In theory this should never happen. If it does you have a major problem and you should use the services of a Unix expert.

```
Incompatible options
```

This error message will display if you have selected the - **n** and the -**s** options at the same time. **fsck** cannot salvage the free list without modifying the file system, but modification is not allowed by the -**n** option. **fsck** will terminate and you can restart it, using one of the two options.

Can't stat root

This is a serious problem. **fsck** cannot get statistics about the root directory. In theory this should never happen, but it has been known to, as shown by the fact that there is an error message. You need the services of the Unix expert, and you will see why they are known as *gurus*.

Can't open check list file

This is not so uncommon an error message, because it can occur when someone has amended or re-written the check list file. The access permissions have been amended and **fsck** has been denied permission to access a file or part of the file system. Check the access permissions on the file and adjust them to the required status for **fsck** to gain access. The utility terminates if it finds this error.

Can't stat [file system name]

The request that **fsck** has made for statistics about the named file system has failed. This system will be ignored and the utility will then continue by checking the next file system named. You should check the access rights to the file system in question.

[filename] is not a block or character device

You have given **fsck** the name of an ordinary file, not of a file system. It will ignore this file, and carry on with the next file system named.

Can't open [file system name]

This is another problem concerned with access rights. **fsck** is unable to open the file system named. It will carry on to the next named file system, and you should again check the access rights.

Size check: fsize x isize y

Here there are two possibilities. Either more blocks are used for the inode list y than there are blocks in the file system, or there are more than 65,535 inodes in the file system. There is no way that **fsck** can deal with this, so it will go on to the next file system.

This message probably means that you have a totally corrupt file system, and you will have to restore it from backup. You might try copying the contents of the file system first, then removing it, and remaking it.

Can't create [file name]

fsck has attempted to create a scratch file, but has failed. This file system will be ignored and **fsck** will proceed to the next.

`Can't seek block n(continue)`

This is another condition that should never arise. There are a good many under Unix. The general advice has to be to see a *guru*.

You can answer *yes* to the question of whether to continue or not, but there is a strong possibility that the condition will recur. The best answer is to enter the response *no* and seek help.

There are two further error messages associated with blocks:
`Cannot read block n(continue)`

and

`Cannot write block n (continue)`

These messages have the same cure: seek help from an expert.

The next set of error messages can arise in phase 1 of running **fsck** .

`Excessive bad blocks I = n (continue)`

More bad blocks than are tolerable have been found. This is usually 10. If you answer *yes* to the request whether to continue or not, it will ignore this inode and proceed with the next inode in the file system.

If this condition has been reported, you will not be able to make a complete check of the file system, and a second run of **fsck** shouild be made to re-check the system.

An answer of *no* here will terminate the running of **fsck**.

`Excessive dup blocks I = n (continue)`

This is similar to the message above, with the only difference being that duplicate blocks have been reported.

`Dup table overflow (continue)`

There is not enough room in the table used by **fsck** to hold the numbers of duplicate blocks. If you give a *yes* answer the program will continue, but any subsequent duplicate blocks will produce the same error and the check will be incomplete. You will have re-run **fsck** to check the file system concerned again. This is the normal procedure.

A *no* response here will terminate the program.

If this error does occur, you should get a systems programmer to amend the source code for your version of **fsck** , giving the utility a larger value to its variable **duptblsize**. The amended source code should then be recompiled with the new object code replacing the old **fsck** object code.

An error message that can arise in phase 2 of running **fsck** is:

```
I out of range I = n name = [file name] (remove)
```

A directory entry with the name [file name] has an inode number which is greater than the end of the free list. If you answer *yes* to the query, asking you whether to remove it or not, the directory entry is removed. If you answer *no*, **fsck** will ignore the error and continue.

It is best to check whether there is any data associated with the directory which be saved by copying it to another file system, and then remove the directory. This will entail giving a *no* response on the first run through and a *yes* response on the second.

14.2 lost+found Directory.

The **lost+found** directory is a special directory, situated in the root directory of the file system, and used by the utility **fsck**.

If any *orphan* files or unconnected directories are found while using **fsck**, there is an option available to reconnect them. If this option is taken, a link will be made between the orphan file or unconnected directory and the **lost+found** directory. The files which appear in this directory do so under their own node number.

There are two specific aspects of the **lost+found** directory which are the particular concern of the system manager: its very existence and its size.

14.2.1 Making the lost+found Directory.

This can be a straightforward task. If there is a shell script called either **mklost+found** or **createl+f**, it is only necessary to run it in order to establish a **lost+found** directory in the system root directory.

The majority of systems, however, do not have these shell-scripts and it is necessary to carry out the following procedure:

-Change directory to the root directory for the file system.

-Make the **lost+found** directory.

-Change directory to **lost+found**.

-Make several directories in the **lost+found** directory, using dummy names.

-Remove the dummy directories.

The process of making and removing dummy directories is necessary in order to make the **lost+found** directory sufficiently large. (A parent directory, such as the **lost+found** directory in this case, is increased in size by having directories made within it, and it remains that size even when such dummy directories are removed.)

The sequence of commands which will create a **lost+found** directory is:

```
$ cd /
$ mkdir lost+found
$ cd lost+found
$ mkdir dummy1
$ mkdir dummy2
$ mkdir dummy3
. . . . .
$ mkdir dummy20
$ rm -ir d*
```

The last command utilises the wild card character, *, in order to remove all the dummy directories within **lost+found** with one command.

The **rm** command is also used with the **-ir** option for good reason. The parameter **-r** enables the **rm** command to be used to remove directories. It is extremely powerful and useful, but potentially dangerous, since it is relatively easy to remove directories which you want to keep and it is therefore sensible to use it in conjunction with the **i** parameter, which makes the command interactive.

There can be no hard and fast rules to indicate how much space a **lost+found** directory should contain. As a rule of thumb, make and remove at least 10 dummy directories.On larger systems it will be necessary to increase this number.

If during the running of **fsck** you see this message:

''SORRY . NO SPACE IN lost+found DIRECTORY

you will need to increase the size of the directory.

On the other hand, do not leave recovered files or directories in the **lost+found** directory. Whenever files or directories have been recovered during **fsck**, check the **lost+found** directory and move the contents to other directories or archives. If this is not done, there will be frequent problems when running **fsck**. It is good practice to check the **lost+found** directory regularly, and to restore as many files to their original place in the system. At the start of fsck, therefore, the **lost+found** directory should be empty.

It is also necessary to set an absolute limit on the time any recovered file can be allowed to remain the **lost+found** directory. The length of this time will depend on the system and how much space is available, but it is recommended that the maximum time is fourteen days before any unrestored files are archived and removed from the **lost+found** directory. Files which have been archived can always be copied back into the system, and it is better to do so, rather than lose valuable data because there is no room in the **lost+found** directory.

Chapter Fifteen
uucp Administration.

There are a large number of network communications programs now being made available on Unix and Unix-like systems. **uucp** is still the most popular, however.

Basically there are three reasons for this. It is part of the standard Unix, as distributed normally. You don't need to go out and buy it specially. It is relatively simple to set up and maintain. Finally it is one of the cheapest networks you can have. If there are two machines fairly close together all you need is a cable to connect them through the appropriate serial ports. If you need to communicate over longer distances, a cheap modem will suffice.

There are a number of operations which have to be carried out, though, before you can use it.

First you must make sure that you have all the files which **uucp** requires, on the system and in the correct directories. This is important because many installations do not use **uucp**, and it has become increasingly the practice of many suppliers to provide the relevant files not on the main distribution disks but on secondary distribution disks. In this way on sites where the facilities are not being used, they are not installed and do not waste even the comparatively small amount of disk space **uucp** requires.

You will require four files to be in the directory /usr/bin. These are **uucp**, **uux**, **uuname** and **uulog**. In addition you will require a directory called /usr/lib/uucp which should contain the files **uucico**, **uuclean**, and **uuxqt**. Finally you will need the home directory for **uucp** which is /usr/spool/uucp. Normally you will have to make this directory and make sure that the ownership is set to **uucp**. You will also have to undertake the operations in the next paragraph before you can change the ownership.

Presuming that you have all the files on your system, you have to make it possible for other systems to log into your system using **uucp**. To do this you will have to set up a user identification for **uucp** by making the appropriate entry in the password and group files. An example of an entry in a the file /etc/passwd is given below:

```
$ uucp::8:2:Unix to Unix:/usr/spool/uucp:
/usr/lib/uucp/uucico
```

It is normal for **uucp** to belong to a group on its own.

The shell program entered by **uucp** is **uucico**, which stands for Unix to Unix copy in copy out program. Systems calling your system through **uucp** expect this program to be started up automatically when they log in.

There is just a small, but vital, point worth noting here: if you look at the entry in the password file you will find that it has no password. Correct this immediately by logging in as **uucp** and using the command **passwd** to change the password.

We have now set up the basic structure for **uucp**. The next step is to set up the environment in which it can work. **uucp** queues files, and we have to make sure that they are sent to other systems. The method normally used to do this is to make an entry in the file **/usr/lib/crontab**. A fairly standard entry would be:

```
5,15,25,35,45,55 * * * * su -uucp -c /usr/lib/uucp/uucico - r1
```

Note that this has been set up to operate every ten minutes. The frequency will depend on the usage of **uucp** and the interval is set to five minutes on many systems, though on a lightly used system it might be set to a longer interval. This is not, however, recommended.

One of the problems with **uucp** is that files can build up in the directory **/usr/spool/uucp**. Fortunately a program, **uuclean**, has been provided to clean these up. It is not always provided, however, on all systems, and where it is not you should write a shell script to undertake the cleaning activities. **uuclean**, or the appropriate shell script, are normally also operated from **cron**. A fairly typical entry is:

```
5 * * * * su - uucp -c /usr/lib/uucp/uuclean -R
```

This will clear the files in **/usr/spool/uucp** that are more than 48 hours old. Note it is set to run every hour at five minutes past the hour. On more lightly used systems this might be run only once or twice a day.

Further cleaning up of the **/usr/spool/uucp** directory is also automatically undertaken by making some additions to the **/etc/rc** file. These are files which can get very large as they have entries made to them every time **uucp** executes any action. There is, however, a problem here. The file **/etc/rc** is executed when the system goes into multi- user mode. If a system is up constantly, **/etc/rc** might not be executed for a considerable period. The incident that triggers it may actually be a system crash, which could be caused by the disk space being completely taken up by the files. Some system managers therefore put these commands in a shell script to be called up daily by **cron**. This is very much a matter for your personal judgement based on experience of your system.

No matter what you decide is correct for your system, the commands are:

```
rm -f /usr/spool/uucp/LCK*
rm -f /usr/spool/uucp/LOGFILE
rm -f /usr/spool/uucp/SYSLOG
```

A point to be kept in mind here is that you may want to examine the log files before removing them. This is particularly important with respect to security checks.

The next stage is to set up a list of users who may make use of **uucp**. This is done by making entries in a file called **/usr/lib/uucp/USERFILE**. The general entry is , /. This gives the broadest access to **uucp**.

In the general entry we have a comma, followed by a space, which is followed by a slash. The actual format for the entry is:

```
[username] , [system name] [directory]
```

Thus the entry , / has no user name specified and no system name specified. These means that any user from any system can use any directory starting at / which is of course the root directory.

A restricted entry might be:

```
, com1 /urs/spool/uucp/public
```

This command restricts any user coming in through the system **com1**, to the directory **/usr/spool/uucp/public**.

It should be noted that there are differences in how versions of **uucp** use the USERFILE, and you should consult your system documentation for the precise method employed on your system.

The next part of the process is to be able to connect to other systems. For this you will need a port with an auto-dial modem attached to it. You will need to make sure that **getty** is turned off for this port. Check the entry in the file **/etc/inittab** for the port and if it is activated replace it with an entry similar to the one below:

```
(ttynum)::off:getty tty(ttynum) !
```

Replace **(ttynum)** with the appropriate entry. Once this is done nobody can log in on that port.

If you are one of those lucky people who have an ACU port on your system, you can ignore the **/etc/inittab** entry if you connect your modem to this port.

Now you have the modem set up, tell the system about it. Information about the specifications of modems is held in the file **/usr/lib/uucp/L-devices**, but please note that some versions of **uucp** use a different name. Again you will have to consult your system documentation.

In this file, **/usr/lib/uucp/L-devices**, each port which can be used for dialing out has one line. Each line contains the following information:

```
device
line
call-unit
speed
```

device is the type of device on a port. The main types of device are **ACU** for Auto Call Unit, **DIR** for Direct hard wired connection and **VEN** for Ven-Tel type automatic-dialing modem.

line is the name of the file in **/dev** for the port. **call-unit** is the automatic-dial unit which is asociated with the port. For hard wired connections this will be zero. For other devices it is normally the same as the line.

Finally there is the speed of data transmission to be set. For modems this will normally be in the range of 300 to 1200. The two normal speeds are 300 and 1200, although an increasing number of 900 baud modems seem to be coming into operation. For hard wired units the speed can go as high as 9600.

A single line in the file **/usr/lib/uucp/L-devices** can therefore look like:

```
ACU tty09 tty09 300
```

Once you have enabled your system to find the modem, and have given it the information to use it, you have to tell it where to call. To call another system you need to have an **id** on that other system, and that is normally **uucp**. You also need to know the password to get onto the system. A further requirement is, of course, the telephone number of the other system. Without this you will have real problems!

For some systems on which public access is encouraged, for example certain information systems, these details are published in the computing press. The probability is,however, that you will want to communicate mainly with other commercial systems, however. In such cases you will have to contact the system manager of the system you wish to connect to and get the information from him or her.

Once you have this information it is included in a file called **/usr/lib/uucp/L.sys**, which contains details about remote systems which your system can call. In this file, **/usr/lib/uucp/L.sys**, each line refers to a remote system and contains the following data:

```
name of remote system
the time when it can be called up
the device to be used to call it
the speed of connection to the remote system
the phone number of the remote system
the login sequence to be used to establish logon
```

name is quite simple: this is the name by which the remote system is known to your system.

Most systems have restrictions on when they will receive calls from other systems. Information on these restrictions is placed in the field for time. A typical entry might be **TuWeTh 1700-1900**. This would mean that the system will receive calls between 5 p.m. and 7 p.m. on Tuesdays, Wednesdays and Thursdays. The code for the days is **Mo,Tu, We, Th, Fr, Sa, Su** for Monday, Tuesday, Wednesday, Thursday, Friday, Saturday and Sunday respectively. The code for any day of the week is **Any**, whilst the days Monday to Friday inclusive can be referred to as weekdays using the code **Wk**. The time is stated using the twenty four hour clock. If no time is given then calls are allowed at any time. Please remember when setting times that you have to allow for time zones if you are using international calls.

device contains either the name of the device as held in the file **/usr/lib/uucp/L devices** or the name of the port when the device is hardwired.

The next field contains the phone number which is to be used for calling the remote system.

Finally comes the login sequence. This is what **uucp** will use to establish the actual login on the remote system. It consists of pairs of words which are separated by blank spaces. The first word in the pair is the message given by the remote system and the second word is the response required from **uucp**.

A fairly common sequence, therefore, is:

```
login: uucp password: public
```

A practice which is often in use is to generate a carriage return on login. In fact this is an absolute requirement sometimes. For instance if you are working on a system which has a modem operating at 300 baud and you are calling a system which is receiving on a modem set to 1200 baud you have a problem. You need to get the modem to switch to 300 baud. This can be done on some modems by sending a carriage return. In place of **login:**, enter:

```
$ login:--login:
```

This will generate an immediate carriage return if the system has not received a **login:** request.

A fairly typical entry in the **/usr/lib/uucp/L.sys** file is:

```
NrthSales Wk ACU 1200 05203433897 gin:--gin:
uucp word: south
```

Here you will note that the words **login:** and **password:** have been abreviated to **gin:** and **word:**. These abreviations are recognised by most versions of **uucp**.

Chapter 16

Staffing.

This chapter deals with a range of issues that concern the system manager and staffing, including staff recruitment, selection, development, and security. It is possible to view these issues as a series of problems which need to be solved. That, however, is not the approach most guaranteed to achieve success. All the points here can be problems, but it is more positive to view them as issues that you can use to your own advantage in running a computer system.

Our starting point is therefore encapsulated in the following sentences. Faced with the complexity of running a modern computer system, it may be easy to overlook the fact that your most valuable resource is your staff. Your staff are your prime concern. Consequently the issues outlined here are vital for the successful management of a computer system.

This chapter is not intended to provide a comprehensive guide to all the personnel management questions and issues that exist, since there are many books which deal very thoroughly with them. What it will do, however, is provide you with a range of significant points that you need to keep in mind when dealing with your staff. In that sense, for example, it is really concerned with the extra issues that face a system manager when dealing with staff matters, rather than an overall view of personnel management. It is also meant to be read in conjunction with the chapter on training, because, in many ways, the two elements are quite closely intertwined.

It may seem strange at first sight to include a security issue in this section, but the reaon for its inclusion will become clear.

16.1 The Background.

The staffing issues that are of particular importance to a system manager are outlined here and will be developed later in a little greater detail. Naturally, these points are written within a slightly wider view, however.

Whatever the state of the wider labour market, there is, inevitably, a shortage in the number of staff who can work happily with a computer system. As more businesses acquire computer installations of one kind or another, more staff have to be found to run them. It is true that the first generation of staff who have been trained at school and college is now starting to reach the labour market, but the figures are still far short of requirements. That fact is likely to be true for at least the next five years in the view of labour market analysts.

In our view, that situation is going to be more or less permanent. To take but one reason: the first generation of school and college leavers who have experience of computer systems are specialists in computer systems. Programming, system analysis and the computers themselves have been the main interest. These people meet one need, but it is not really the commercial need for people who can use computer systems in a commercial environment. Special programs in education, such as the British Technical and Vocational Educational Initiative (TVEI) are beginning to alter that situation, but only in limited areas and ways.

Against this background of a more or less permanent shortage of properly trained staff, then, the following special factors that apply to a computer system staff need to be viewed.

Working with a computer system is extremely labour intensive. That seems a paradox in view of the job erosion caused by the introduction of computers, but in reality it is not. While, undoubtedly, many jobs have disappeared through the introduction of computerised methods, the jobs that have remained, or been created by that same process, have become, if anything, more labour intensive.

Secondly, the people who work with computer systems must be highly skilled, usually in two ways. Not only must they be intellectually skilled, but, for the present at least, they must be able to use a keyboard effectively. Thus you must have staff who are capable in both areas and the two do not always go together!

Thirdly, there is obviously a real premium on knowledge and skills in using a computer system for all staff working on computer systems, but the real key to successful people within data processing is a very high degree of resourcefulness. As you will no doubt have seen for yourself, the successful people working with a computer system must not only know the correct answer, but they must also be capable of working out, on their own usually, what to do when the right answer does not work. That ability includes the determination to sort things out for themselves, which is the fourth special quality.

Previously, when working with a computer system, there were nearly always experts around to ask when things went wrong, or were not working as expected. Nowadays, each person, except in the largest establishments, will rapidly become the person who is most expert at any particular job involving the computer. There will be some duplication and you will have ensured that there are always people available to deputise. At the same time, however, no deputy will know as much as the person directly responsible. (This is a further reminder that all procedures and activities should be carefully logged so that you build up a basic knowledge of the computer system, which can be shared when necessary.) It is likely, after all, that there just will not be any answers available, except the answers that someone working on that particular job can find. Your staff will need to be able to take on that responsibility.

Fifthly, as an extension of this ability, you need staff who are self-motivating. There will be any number of mundane tasks, on the level of fairly simple drudgery, when working with a computer system. For instance, data entry and compilation is hardly the most stimulating activity. On the other hand, even the lowliest data entry clerk can make a difference if sufficiently motivated to solve immediately any problems that occur.

A sixth special factor is an absolutely paramount requirement: staff loyalty. All businesses need it to prosper, but can survive if it isn't total. Managing a computer system becomes absolutely impossible without loyalty, extremely difficult if the loyalty is not total, and relatively easy if you have it. In a sense, the first requirement is total loyalty of the system manager to his or her staff. But the second requirement is always total staff loyalty to the company and department.

Finally, part of the work will always be performed against very tight deadlines, imposed on the department by the other departments it serves. Staff will need to be very flexible in their approach to working hours, because such deadlines do not often respect the actual needs of working with a computer system.

16.2 Staff Shortage.

For the reasons given above, the likelihood of a shortage of the right staff is both a fact of life and an incentive to get your staff relationships right. Oscar Wilde wrote an extremely short but quite comprehensive treatise on economics, which said that where there is supply there is no demand; where there is demand, there is no supply. It is much better to be involved in an area where there is demand!

It is usual to start an analysis of the staffing issues of any company with the question of recruitment. Within the area of working with a computer system, the real starting point is retaining your staff. There are always people that you can quite happily let go. But if you take the view that your main asset is your staff, then your first priority will be in keeping the good people you already have.

Clearly you will know the usual personnel management responses to retaining good staff, like involving your staff fully, being seen to be involved yourself, communicating with your staff formally and informally, making sure they know what is going on in the company as a whole, giving them proper tools to do the job, providing proper training, creating a career structure, offering rewards and promotion and generally being concerned about pay and conditions.

All of these are important and usually well-known, but we want to draw attention to one of the above, which does tend to become ignored within the self-contained world of data processing. That is, of course, making sure that your staff knows what is going on within the wider realm of the company. While a successful accountancy package is doubtless a joy in itself, it does become much more interesting if it is related to the overall success, failures and needs of the company. Working with a computer system can become very inward-looking, and needs this extra dimension.

The point at issue here is retaining your good staff, and how to achieve that aim. Remembering the special issues that apply to staff running a computer system which we identified, you will know that your staff are more than usually intelligent, capable and resourceful. In order to retain them, you have to believe in them.

The first answer is to work out whether you do wish to retain them. It is not for nothing that we have been discussing retaining *good staff*. Thus the first question you must answer is whether you really do value your staff. If the answer is no, you need a far more fundamental analysis of your own situation than can be suggested here, though you might pick up some guidelines for further thought.

Assuming, therefore, that your answer is positive, the first step is to show your staff that you take this view. We have heard it said that this is obvious, meaning both that the attitude must be obvious to the staff and that this is an obvious thing to do. In neither case can anyone assume that it is obvious. The point needs to be made and made more than once.

Paradoxically, retaining your staff may also depend on knowing when it is appropriate for them to leave. We all know that advancement can be quicker if people change firms and gain a greater width of knowledge. If your staff know that you have their greater welfare at heart and are prepared to take into account their particular careers, you may well find that you gain greater respect, retain your staff longer and get greater commitment.

Secondly, your training and retraining program needs to be geared both to your departmental needs and the needs of your staff, as is dealt with in the section on training.

Thirdly, if anyone leaves, find out why they are leaving. This sounds obvious but it can be forgotten and, in fact, you cannot take the first answer that anyone gives. Asked this question most people will mention money or conditions. Pushed a bit further, without ignoring the fact that the reasons already given may well be correct, you will probably obtain a better insight into how your department is perceived by your staff. At that point you can consider taking remedial action if you think it is appropriate.

Fourthly, you will need to keep an eye on the general market in your area. This again sounds obvious, but it is more difficult than it sounds, especially faced with the problems of running a Unix or Unix-like machine!

These general statements imply a great deal of commitment, but the one that we insist is the most important is the first: that you work out for yourself whether you do regard your staff as your most valuable asset. Everything else flows from there.

16.3 Staff Recruitment and Selection.

No matter how good you are at retaining your staff, even if no other factors were involved it would be unhealthy if no-one ever left and no-one new ever arrived. We have already mentioned being aware of when a person should leave for that person's benefit. You should always, therefore, be recruiting, even when you are not actively engaged in seeking staff. It is an attitude of mind: working out what you need to do to attract good staff, how the market is changing, and how your needs within the computer system are changing.

After all, new factors will be continually arising. The computer system will not remain the same for ever. New tasks will be developed, new skills demanded. New equipment may arrive. At the same time, all these may be either replacements for what you have already, or additional items. Training and retraining, even if planned and implemented effectively, will not alone mean that there are no outstanding issues.

On the other hand, you may be setting up a new department. In this case, recruitment is immediately a burning issue. Just as with an established department, recruitment is not something you will ever stop doing, even, let it be said, when the department contracts in staff numbers! That eventuality itself creates so many new factors that, for a start, you will probably not have the right staff left.

Whatever else, then, recruitment is a major element in your work as a system manager. If you work within a large company, you will obviously have fully-formed company policies over using advertisements or employment agencies. If you work with a smaller company, these may well be issues for you to decide. Once again the purpose of this discussion is not to settle these major issues, but to give some pointers in the right direction.

Using an agency to find suitable staff is immediately attractive, especially if the agency performs initial screening of candidates. Some do not do this and it is difficult to see what function they have in that case. There is an overhead: typically an agency will charge between one month and three months' salary for finding the right person. Compared with your own costs, however, this may well be cost-effective, particularly if the agency is well-versed in the data processing area.

Alternatively, you can place advertisements yourself and carry out the initial screening, against such factors as qualifications, age and experience.

Either way, there is no substitute for your first step, which must be to draw up your requirements. To do this you need to write a full job description, state your requirements in terms of qualifications and experience, give an age range, and then add the level of salary and the types of conditions that will apply. (At this point, particularly within a large company, you may well need to insist to higher management on the differences in working with a computer system, particularly in terms of work patterns.) In addition you will need to identify all the elements that might make the post attractive to the right person: location, facilities, system being used and any other factors.

The first key issue is the job description: what do you really want the person to do? If you, like most people, have been appointed to jobs to find that you were doing something only marginally related to what you were employed to do, you will know how poorly written most job descriptions are. Since this will initially be a private document, be honest with yourself. In most cases you will have a specific task for someone to do, but that will only be part of the story. Add the rest of the description, however vague it is. If you want someone who, in addition to being a first class user of word processing equipment, must be able to get printers to work, make sure it says that. Even these two skills rarely go together. If you are vague about what you will want the person to do after the first six months, make that clear, at least to yourself. It will help when you come to screening applications.

You will also need to specify how you want the applications: a letter, a form filled in; accompanied by a curriculum vitae or a resume; a description of past activities; references. A brief word of guidance: forms will make your life easier; letters may well be more helpful.

Secondly you need to sort out the question of qualifications and experience. No doubt when you first started applying for posts for your own career you will have had the common experience of reading job advertisements that required a 21 year old, with a Ph.D in the exact specialism under discussion, with a minimum of ten years appropriate experience in industry and a wide range of other essential assets. This is obviously laughable, but examples abound. The lesson is that you should be very clear about what qualifications and experience you want and need. In the area of data processing you may not want a specialist, for example. You may well not be able to get someone with what you consider the right qualifications. You have to ask yourself what you want as a minimum and by that, what you need before you can appoint someone. Taking into account the special factors in this area, it may well be that you want someone who is adaptable and capable of learning, rather than someone who knows a great deal. At the very least, be highly critical of your first responses.

Thirdly you need to specify an age range to be fair to candidates and yourself. Whatever figures you arrive at, you need to be able to justify them and not require twenty years experience from a 25 year old! Is experience of life an important factor, or is a new brain unsullied by past experience what you need?

When it comes to screening applications you will inevitably have to do so against your requirements, so it is wise to get that right first! Thus when you receive applications, your job will be much simplified if you specified the requirements properly. As you read applications, however, be prepared to revise your requirements and re-evaluate your needs.

Interviewing is a skilled job: look on it as such. Most people tend to see interviewing candidates as a one-way process: gaining information about a candidate. The successful interviews are those in which a genuine conversation takes place. For a start a candidate will be much more forthcoming and less guarded. Secondly you will learn whether the candidate feels you have anything to offer. After all, what you are looking for is some form of partnership. It is not enough for you to feel that you have got the right person, unless the person feels he or she has got the right job.

We would place the qualities we think you should be looking for in the following order: the ability of the candidate to fit into a team, while still being resourceful and willing, and capable of thinking and learning. As we said data processing is labour intensive and your staff need to be able to get with each other, more than they probably need to get on with the computer system. A mixture of skills and abilities must be demonstrated: both intellectual and manual dexterity are important. The appropriateness of qualifications, background and experience should be last, since a good candidate should be able to acquire all these and only a bad candidate will rely on them to succeed.

Make notes at the interview about the candidates, both what impresses you and what you regard as drawbacks to their application. This will help when you come to make the decision to appoint or not.

When it comes to appointing, by far the best way is to establish three or four categories within which you can place the candidates. The easiest one to deal with is those you do not wish to employ, for whatever reason. If this means that certain people are eliminated, it will make choosing the right person easier.

Secondly, consider whether there are any candidates who are not really suitable for the current post, but for whom there could well be an opening later. That will also help both the current task, and later recruitment.

Thirdly, reverse the procedure, and ask yourself are there any candidates that you definitely want to appoint. That will cut through any number of problems. If there is more than one, you can continue from here, by establishing the advantages and disadvantages of each in turn. Do not make a decision at this point, unless you have eliminated all the other candidates.

Fourthly, which candidates are you doubtful about: re-assess your own views and see whether the doubts arise because of your initial requirements or whether it is a substantial drawback. Ask yourself whether obtaining references would help - and if so, how. If there is no substantial drawback to any of these candidates, add them to the third list.

Then you can make your decision, taking the broadest possible view, having assessed the special abilities you require. But once you have made your decision, write down your reasons, so that you have a record for later.

Finally, after six months, review your job description, your initial requirements, and the salary and conditions you offered. Then review the successful candidate's application, and the notes you made at the interview. This will help you in further recruiting and in understanding precisely what your department is doing, as opposed to what you might think it is! Self-criticism, in private, is very healthy in terms of recruitment.

16.4 Staff Security.

Much of what has been written in this chapter leads naturally to this section: security. It is probably a shock to realise it but most breaches in system security do not originate outside the installation. Most are carried out by staff who have legitimate access to the system.

Many employers are very concerned about the problem of breaches of security by staff and are going to quite long lengths to prevent such breaches. Some of the reports from America about the steps being taken there are amazing. It seems that some employers are put at risk by their staff but put more at risk by a growing number of security specialists. Without getting that extreme, it is worth being aware of the dangers.

The Unix operating system has any number of security devices built into it. In fact, partly what makes it such a pain to use is the fact that it is oriented so closely towards security. Yet there is no perfect security device. However complex you make your system, however unpleasant or impossible to use it becomes, your system will never be absolutely secure. If a person set up the security, then someone else can break that protection. In fact, the more secure it is, the more of a challenge it is!

There is one answer, however. The most secure system is that in which you can trust your staff implicitly, without ever having to. That is, take all the appropriate steps to secure your system, but at the same time, you will have to rely on your staff's loyalty in the end. The corollary is that as soon as you can no longer be sure about the loyalty of a member of staff, that member of staff must be denied access to the system. The basic rule is that if at any time members of staff hand in their notice, or you give notice to a member of staff, from that moment on they should not have access to the system.

There is more to this than just protecting the system. It also protects the member of staff. All too often when errors arise on systems, such errors are blamed on staff members who were serving out notice periods at the time when they were entered into the system.

On the positive side, however, as a system manager you must address yourself to the task of developing and maintaining staff loyalty. This means that you must also develop an attitude of trust by your own senior management towards the computer department. Too often senior managers feel that the computer department and staff are a law unto themselves. Where such attitudes exist the computer staff will feel that they are not trusted and therefore will not give loyalty in return. This comes back to the point about involving your staff, too, in the wider framework of the company.

When you think of all the sensitive information that is on your system, from marketing plans and results, to salaries and addresses, you will start to have a very real grasp of the dangers involved. Yet the answer is to be positive and not to introduce any of the deterrent measures, such as lie detectors and other such paraphernalia that are being recommended in America. If your staff are loyal and recognise that their interests lie in preserving the security of the computer system the problem becomes far simpler.

As we said the biggest danger is from internal breaches of security. If you can prevent that by taking a positive attitude towards your staff, you will have defeated the biggest danger. In turn, the threat from outside becomes reduced, because the safeguards built into Unix and Unix-like systems, if properly implemented by you and your staff, will deflect all but the most determined thief.

16.5 Conclusion.

Your staff members should be your most valuable asset. Treat them as such and your job is much easier. More than that, your job becomes possible. If your staff are not with you, your role as system manager becomes impossible. It seems a simple choice put like that!

Chapter Seventeen
The System Manager and Training.

17.1 Introduction.

An essential concern of the system manager is training both him or herself and training the staff who will be using the system. Training and retraining is time-consuming and expensive. On the other hand, untrained staff can wreak havoc, and cause far more expensive damage than the cost of their training. Accordingly, it is one of the system manager's tasks to make sure that there is a proper and effective training program.

Such a program needs to be planned in just the same way as the rest of the system if it is to be both cost-effective and successful. Moreover, it is not a once and for all cost: training will actually cover retraining staff as well, both as the staff move on to different tasks and as they need to use different applications.

When specifying and ordering a computer system, training requirements and costs should be included in the specification. It cannot be seen as a luxury that may be provided if it can be fitted into the existing budget. The damage that a naive user without proper training can do to a system can be immense - far more than the cost of adequate training.

It is not entirely fanciful therefore to make the decision about which particular computer system to buy on the basis of the documentation and training provided with it. At the very least, if you leave this element out of the specification of a new system, you may well have cause for regret. In many cases, indeed, the equipment on offer may well be very similar, and the only difference between the various systems may be the quality of the documentation and training.

Such variations in the quality of the documentation can be valuable pointers to the quality of the whole system. Whether the manuals are proper books, with full colour illustrations, for example, may not be important, except that they can show you the relative weight attached to documentation by the system manufacturer or supplier. The most important aspect, naturally, is how the manuals are written and they should be examined very critically. For example, the first question you must ask yourself is who the documentation is aimed at, and how successful it is in addressing its audience. Further guidance on what to look for when assessing the quality and effectiveness of documentation will be given later in this section. Good documentation, after all, is the cornerstone of effective training.

This chapter is intended to give and illustrate guidelines for the proper provision of training of staff working with computers. It is also concerned with explaining why such training is important. Finally it will give a checklist for the system manager, so that he or she can plan the training that is required.

Training can have many unexpected problems and certainly a large number of pitfalls. As you read this chapter, you will have to be self-critical as well as being aware of the range of opportunities and possibilities under discussion. You may, for example, create what appears to be a perfect training system and yet still find that it is not very effective. The difference between effective and ineffective training may in the end come down to something as apparently intangible as the atmosphere within which the system is used. Creating the right atmosphere is therefore what this chapter is about more than anything else. The analysis and the approach is here to provide that vital ingredient. It is based on many years experience of training and learning and has a basic philosophy which may seem obvious, but which is vital.

The philosophy behind the training schemes outlined here is quite simply based on reward. Reward itself can mean many things. In this approach the rewards may exist simply within the training scheme itself - offering, for example, the chance to gain access to more of the system. On the other hand, it is worth considering whether more tangible rewards also ought to be built into your training program.

Whatever form the rewards take, the idea is to give people an incentive to train themselves and to become proficient users. This is by far the most effective approach. Even by recording and recognising the standard of training achieved by your staff you will have injected reward into your training scheme. On the other hand, if you only record the standards achieved, you will have undermined the whole approach. You can include many forms of recognition within the training scheme. For example, movement between different levels of training should be related to performance, and greater access to parts of the system, mentioned above, can also be used as a recognition of progress. Such internal rewards ought to be supplemented in order to create an environment where training is held in esteem.

As you read this chapter you may well think that training is assuming too big a part of the overall time given to managing a computer system. It is probably possible to acquire a training- for-training's-sake mentality, but the dangers in that are far outweighed by the danger to a system of badly or partly trained staff. Nevertheless, what is written here does not go much beyond what we could consider a bare minimum of effort in order to make an effective program. If you still have doubts, consider how much time you spend answering questions about the system, anyway. If your training is effective, that overhead should be removed, at the very least!

It may well be that certain aspects of this section are only of marginal concern to you, but it is probably worth considering all the elements in order to give yourself a touchstone which you can use when you analyse your own requirements.

17.2 Initial Steps.

In order to be able to identify what your training program ought to comprise, the first question that you have to ask yourself is what you hope to achieve. It is worth looking at two aspects of your role when you are formulating your answer to this question.

The first aspect should involve a firm analysis of the requirements your staff have and create. It could be, for example, that you have a large number of temporary staff, for whom large-scale training is both expensive and self-defeating. Equally, you may have a department which has a high staff turnover. Your training needs are going to be very different in that case from those in a department where there is a relatively stable staff.

Secondly you need to examine the requirements imposed on you and your staff by the type of equipment you will be using. If the system that you are managing is likely to remain more or less as it is for the next few years, both in its application programs and its hardware, you are in a very different situation from the system manager who has to take account of frequent changes in hardware, including peripheral devices like printers, and frequent changes in the application programs at the heart of the system.

Incidentally, since most major manufacturers and suppliers tend to regard five years as the time in which they are prepared to support and maintain their equipment and programs, what constitutes a relatively stable system is perhaps open to question. It is easier to approach the problem by asking whether there are significant changes to your system at greater frequency, on average, than six months. If the interval is greater than this, you have a fairly stable system; if it is less than this, obviously it is best to consider that you are facing a very difficult problem.

One way of tackling such a problem is to isolate the areas where change occurs most frequently and to treat those separately, always trying to preserve a core of standard training which you know will not become outdated too quickly. By concentrating your resources in the more stable areas, you will probably find that the areas in which rapid changes take place can be allowed for without too much disruption.

To answer the question at the start of this section is not possible in general terms. However, you might like to consider which of the following most closely match what you are trying to achieve:

- A minimum level of expertise across the staff and a pool of more experienced or more highly trained staff to act as immediate help and replacement if needed.

- Rigidly defined boundaries both between tasks and between users of the system, with high levels of expertise within narrow areas, allowing very little overlap of skills.

- General expertise right across the staff, and an awareness of the basic elements of most areas in nearly all staff members.

- Constant training and retraining, so that the staff are immediately capable of taking on any of the tasks right across the system - including deputising for you.

These categories of answers are relatively crude, and may not apply exactly to your position. Nevertheless, they do cover most of the possibilities - and it is likely, for example, that all system managers will have someone who can deputise for them, at least if they are prudent! As you will probably have seen, these categories also indicate greater training costs as you move from the first to the last. This chapter is not designed to ignore that vital area of your responsibility. Clearly, you need to have the most cost-effective training program. You can only have that if you are sure you know what you want and what to achieve.

17.3 Three Levels in Training.

Having decided what your goals are in creating a training program, you need to consider how to divide up the training process, so that it can be properly planned. Not all trainees will be at the same position when they start, and, indeed, not all systems and offices are the same.

Training - and training also stands for retraining throughout this chapter - has three main levels whether for hardware, software or the use of the whole system: introduction, consolidation and using more advanced features. Naturally the dividing line between these three will be hard to distinguish both at the level of introducing new applications and procedures and training particular individuals.

In planning your training, you will find it useful to have two different planning schemes: a public and a private version of what is going on. Your private one ought to be based on the three tier approach, since this determines the type of training that should be given. Your public version of training will include many more levels. The reasons behind this are psychological, because, as mentioned earlier, you will want to build incentive and reward into your training program, and the simplest direct way is to include progress up a ladder of achievements with finely graded steps.

It is worth noting that many formal training companies provide very short introductory courses coupled with many more courses which are labelled "intermediate". They have found over the years that no-one really likes to be seen as a naive user, and the sooner the course is called intermediate the better it is attended. In one case, a training establishment which specialised in introductions to software applications actually abandoned calling any of its courses "introductory" and called them all intermediate level. The courses remained exactly the same, but the attendance increased dramatically.

The correct approach is to have very short introductory training, followed by many consolidating "intermediate" levels, where people are gaining the essential skills they need for using the system effectively. At the same time, these intermediate levels need to be graded - at least in appearance.

Having grasped the three basic levels in training, it is necessary to divide each stage further, so that you can form an effective outline of the training you want to provide. At each of the three levels of training, introduction, consolidation and advanced, the training can be divided into four parts. These are the introduction of concepts, the skills involved in using the concepts, using the concepts in practice and finally evaluating how well the person has understood and used the concepts involved. This final stage may seem self-evident, or catered for by the fact that each individual will be actually using the system. That this is not the case will become apparent as this section advances.

Part of the research work that has been done into how people learn about computer systems has centered on the fact that individuals form models of the system they are using. This happens very quickly - certainly within the first few hours of its use. What then happens is that even where certain elements of the system are in conflict with, or directly contradicted by, the person's own model, the model somehow remains intact. The model is in fact confirmed by the experience of using the system, rather than being modified to coincide with reality. This can have extremely odd results, which may not be apparent unless formal evaluation of what has been learnt, and how it has been learnt, is built into the system.

It becomes important to approach the training of your staff knowing how the training is perceived by them. In fact, if you can impose the main elements of your model of the system in your training, you will probably be much more effective - as long as your own model of how the system works and functions is relatively correct! This is where a certain element of self- criticism is important.

Knowing who is going to train your staff is obviously important. It is also important to know how your training staff have been trained. When we get to the section on choosing formal training approaches, this will be developed in detail. At the moment it is merely important to keep it in mind.

The four stages of learning outlined here should seem like commonsense, although they are not universally adopted. The first objection may be to starting with the concepts to be imparted. Some people like to start with actual practice, find out what a person is doing wrong and then correct that. The danger in this approach can readily be appreciated, particularly at the levels of what sort of model is being formed by the person being trained.

To take a concrete example. To introduce trained typists to word processing, it is quite feasible to start the system, place the keyboard in front of them and watch them type. As and when errors occur, or there is a need to add a new skill, like deleting a character or line, the trainer can intervene. In many training courses this is exactly what happens. The results may not be immediately bad, but one effect is that people actually have more difficulty remembering how to do things. You might care to experiment with this idea to see how true it is. What happens is that every time a function comes up, it has to be referred to, or even thought through by going back to what the person was doing when last trying to accomplish it. This can be a very time-consuming process and very unproductive, though unless you were looking for it, it might pass unnoticed.

On the other hand, the concept based approach is much more structured, so that individual functions and skills are related to an overall view of how to approach the task in hand, such as word processing. It is fairly easy to demonstrate this by examining how word processing is actually first perceived as different from using a typewriter by a trained typist.

However odd it may seem, many people fail for a long time to grasp that the fundamental element of word processing which distinguishes it from using any typewriter, is that it separates the function of creation from that of editing and production. Once this has been understood, however, it can have a dramatic impact on how productive a person is. Trained typists generally, almost subconsciously recognise when a typing error has occurred. If they are unused to word processing they will probably correct errors immediately after they occur. In many cases, however, this is time-consuming and a denial of the advantages of word processing. Since errors will inevitably arise that the typist will not notice, some form of proof-checking is essential once the complete document has been typed. It is probably quicker nine times out of ten to do all error corrections in one process. This is particularly true if some form of spelling check is included in the application program. Yet there are many people who are competent users of word processing systems, who never grasp this fundamental point and while they appear to be productive, the likelihood is that they are performing below their capabilities.

Of course it is often argued that whatever suits the individual is best and this does have some truth. On the other hand, the people who generally make this type of response have usually unthinkingly adopted the approach that is being criticised, and feel under attack. They therefore defend their own practice rather irrationally.

This is where it is important to evaluate your own practice self- critically, so that your model of the system is actually both correct and effective. We all have our individual quirks and fancies - in data processing no less than in any other subject.

The benefits of the concept-based approach, however, are revealed in more than just eliminating bad practice and are concerned with stopping that bad practice from the start. As was said earlier, you should be aware that you are creating a model of the system consciously or unconsciously, as your staff learn. Creating your own structured model will help your staff learn very much better, as individual elements can all be related, or associated, with a particular understanding of the system. This in turn encourages retention of knowledge. You are probably well aware yourself of certain aspects of your work which you have to check every time you want to do them. It may be that you have not fully understood the concepts that lie behind what you are doing and so have no way of linking those particular processes to the rest of your work.

To return to the question of error checking: it is useful to divide the functions in any particular word processing system into those specifically designed to assist creation of documents, such as word-wrap and initial format commands, from those that facilitate editing such as block movements and search and replace. This may seem like so much commonsense. We hope it does, but we know that all too often it is not applied. By creating such a structured approach, at even such an elementary level, you will be creating a course which is easily remembered and which also meets the criteria laid down in the three levels of training.

In slightly more detail, this is how the three stages can be perceived in teaching a trained typist to become a skilled word processing computer operator.

The introductory stage has four parts. The first is conveying what makes word processing different from and superior to ordinary typing. The second part might explore how the person being trained can immediately see the advantages of separating creation from final production. Thirdly, by asking them to type a document, paying little attention to either mistakes or the overall format of the document you will be confirming and reinforcing your initial approach. This will be especially true for a trained typist who will probably find it very difficult not to stop and make corrections while typing. The final part of the first stage is to talk through with the person being trained what they have learned, in order to see whether they have grasped what you have been trying to say. If they have, they are immediately rewarded by moving onto the intermediate level or second stage.

The second stage is the one which you may wish to break up into many shorter elements in order to provide the motivation already discussed. It will be centered on correcting and editing the document that was originally produced in the first stage, and then formatting it for final copies. The first stage can be an explanation of the various processes that are available so that text can be edited and produced as a final document, including, for example, automatic page numbering, changing the tabulation of paragraphs and proof-reading. As each item is explained, and fitted into your overall model, it can be used by the trainee. This process will inevitably encompass most of the usual word processing functions, like block movements, page formats, search and replace, and use of other formatting commands like double strike and underline.

At each point in the intermediate stage the concept of word processing, the separation of creation from editing and production, should be reinforced. At the end of each session, you can evaluate how well both your training program and how well the person is doing both by discussing the skills that have been taught and by setting exercises which should be directly related to the person's every day work. If these are chosen skillfully, they will also have the beneficial effect of persuading the person concerned how much easier their job is as a result of using a word processing system.

Finally, once the person has shown competence and an understanding of the essential elements of using a word processor, more advanced features, such as creating "boiler- plate" letters and merged reports can be taught. At this level, the introduction of these concepts can usually be most effectively accomplished through discussion, asking the people being trained what further features would make their work easier. If the discussion is led properly, the idea of "boiler- plate" paragraphs and merged letters, for example, will occur to your staff, to be incorporated into the practical sessions.

It can be objected that such a heavily structured and carefully analysed approach can seem highly artifical and be seen as stifling both individual initiative and creativity. To meet such objections, however, it is only necessary to look at the alternative, which is unstructured and haphazard, relying on the whims and prejudices of the person doing the training. Of course the calibre of those you choose to do the training is very important - a poor trainer can ruin even the most carefully organised scheme, while a first class trainer can breathe life into the most outrageously erratic training session. The advantage that this approach does offer the system manager, however, is that it will give you a standardised course which you can assess independently each time it is given. It will also help the average trainer achieve greater than average results. Even a first class trainer will do better with such a skeleton course, because such a trainer will know both what to expect of the trainees and what is expected of the training course.

17.4 Types of Trainees.

It is essential when planning your training program to know how to classify your trainees. In practice, we have found it useful to consider that there are four main types of trainee. The first are those who are completely naive users. The second are those that have a basic knowledge, but who need training in specific areas. The third are those who are experienced users but who need to use a new function within an application program, or those who need a refresher course. Finally there are the experienced users of one system who are transferring to a new system.

The point of making these classifications is not to shoe-horn people into categories, but to help you sort out priorities in your training. It is part of the overall plan of providing you with the best possible, and that includes cost-effective of course, training. Inevitably there will be people who do not quite fit into any of these categories, or people who bridge two or three of them. This approach is, however, very flexible and can take account of this variation. Once you have decided what types of trainees you have to cater for, you will have to decide what their needs are.

Basically there are three types of situation into which each of these groups may fall. The first is the people who need to be trained to use a specific application or range of applications. The second group is those who need that knowledge, or some subset of it, but who also need to have a certain background in using the system itself. The third group are those who may well need some training in individual applications, but whose main need is to be able to operate the system competently.

In this way, you have to cater for twelve different categories in theory at least, and probably about six or seven in practice, since the overlap that will occur between these divisions will not always be very important.

You may well find it useful to draw up a matrix and place each of the members of the staff who will be using the system within it. This will very quickly show you what the needs are, and more importantly perhaps, what the priorities are.

There is one further element that you will need to consider, however. It is perhaps the most difficult, mainly because it is almost unrelated to the computer system itself. It is likely, though, that it will cause enough difficulties. This element is considering the level of your trainees within the company itself.

There will inevitably be variations in response to training from people as individuals within a company, but the various grades of staff will very often have different approaches to training. For example, you may well have to face with your managers what have become the usual problems with managers who need to use the system. They may want to use the system but hold firmly to one of two views. The first is that they should be capable of using the system intuitively, almost because they see this as a reflection of their intelligence or their rank in the company. The second view is that they have no time to plod through any training and they are not even prepared to read any documentation at all, except as a very last resort. In some cases both views are held at the same time. This sounds extreme, but is often found in practice! It may seem paradoxical that such an attitude can be held by the very person who sees the merits of a full and comprehensive training scheme for the rest of the staff, but it is often the case.

Such views and attitudes represent a very real danger. Not only can the process of learning how to use the system be unnecessarily lengthened, but a naive user can cause quite significant damage to data. The secret here is to design your training system to take account of such people and attitudes and to work round them, effectively making sure that training is provided for them, without it being too apparent. That can be done in a variety of ways, some of which can be very labour- intensive. It is possible, for example, to make sure that during the period in which a manager is being introduced to a new system or application, the person the manager is working with is fully conversant with the system and can train the manager as the system is being used. The person to give the training obviously needs to be chosen with care, but it is often a satisfactory solution.

Another, more drastic way, is to appear to accept that the manager is right, and leave him or her to get on with it, after carefully restricting access to the system beforehand.

The point to be grasped here is that there are many problems in training people to use a system. The answer is very often to be flexible. In the example just given, the solution is very labour intensive - with one-to-one training being given. The alternative, however, may well be to accept significant damage to the system itself. The relative costs involved start to make sense put that way. Naturally, if the manager is trained in the system properly, whether almost subliminally or not, and given a proper model of the system, the benefits may well be long standing. And at the point where you feel the manager is properly trained, it is worth pointing out to him or her exactly what you have done. Otherwise the manager may assume that since he or she required no training, no-one else does! In training, therefore, the answer is to take a broad view of the problems, and apply very specific solutions.

The advantages of dividing your trainees into different categories, at least when producing your training scheme, is that you can quickly start to understand what type of training is required.

If much of the work on your system involves data entry within rigidly defined formats, there is probably no need for lengthy analysis. If, however, it starts to be more complex than that, and you have to consider what happens if key people are on holiday or go sick, such careful analysis will repay the time and effort.

17.5 Types of Training.

There are basically four types of training, and this chapter will cover three of them in detail. In addition, there are some guidelines here on how to assess the quality of the documentation supplied with your system. It is part of this approach to training to see good documentation as the cornerstone of good training, and that is where this section will start.

The first type of training is that which can be called blundering through. The second type of training is on-line training, where the course and information is held on the computer system itself. The third is using self-study materials, of which this book could be considered partly representative. (There is no evaluation of the reader's understanding or abilities, so it is not really a fullly fledged training scheme.) Fourthly, there is formal, classroom based training.

A major element in any training scheme will be the documentation that has been supplied with the system or the application programs. In all forms of training, these manuals are a vital resource. When specifying and ordering a system, it is essential that an evaluation of the manuals themselves is also carried out. Very often the people who do this will not have a very clear idea about the standards that should be applied, so the following checklist should be kept in mind. It does not pretend to be the final word, but it will guide you in the right direction. (It cannot be universal because of the varying nature of the demands that will be placed on manuals, in particular how adaptable and capable your staff are. On the other hand, even in extreme cases, these guidelines will provide a starting point.)

We said earlier that it is a good idea to look at the physical aspects of the manuals. It may well not be a good indication of the contents of the manuals if they have been written using a near draft quality printer and badly photocopied, and stuck, loose, in a folder. It is, however, a good indication of the value placed on the manuals by the manufacturer or supplier! If the documentation is presented properly, it is usually reasonable to assume that the supplier is concerned about providing decent reference and guidance manuals. On the other hand, I have seen cases where the superb quality of the four colour pictures and excellent binding and boxed sets were used almost to cover up the fact that the manuals themselves were useless.

One important aspect, relevant to this point, is how durable the manuals are. It is likely that the documentation supplied will receive fairly intensive use - if it does not, it may well be very indicative that either the system or the documentation is poor! Nevertheless, check that the documentation is durable enough so that it can withstand constant use. Checking that you receive an adequate number of copies is also very important.

Secondly the documentation must be evaluated by checking its content. In the first place, it has to be accurate. If it describes the system as it was, rather than as it is now, then it is probably worse than useless, and an actual hazard. Indeed, almost worse than no documentation at all. It is probably obvious that it is necessary to try some of the more complicated aspects of the system, following to the letter what the documentation says. On the other hand, it is equally important to try some of the simpler tasks, following exactly what the manual says, and making no adjustments on the grounds that you know what the manual is really saying. The reason for this is that, taking a relatively simple task, you will readily see if the manuals are wrong, and have a good idea of how serious the errors are. It is important here that a knowledgeable person carries out this evaluation, but a person who is capable of being as bloody-minded as possible. Do be aware, however, that most people who already know what should be happening read that meaning into the documentation, even where it plainly does not say what is really to be done. Find someone who is either very good at being bloody-minded or is very good at just following rules. Most firms will have such a person, who always follows instructions to the letter, even where the instructions are plainly wrong. Such people do have a use, if only in this area.

The third aspect of evaluation of the content involves assessing who the manuals are aimed at, and checking whether such people can in fact follow what is being written. Each manual should identify, in its preface or introduction, what it is intended to convey and who it is intended for. It should then meet the needs of its intended audience. A manual which has been written for a naive user should, for example, explain all the terms as they are encountered, as well as providing an index and glossary. There should be a proper flow through the manual, starting with the initial concepts and skills and progressing towards the goal outlined at the beginning. The best approach here is to allow a typical user from each of the types identified to try to use the documentation. In addition, you should be aware that although it is not significant initially if the system manager's manual is unreadable by a naive user, it may well turn out that in time the naive user will have to read and understand that manual. The type of concepts involved and how they are explained thus become very significant.

Every piece of documentation should reach certain minimum standards, then. It should contain a table of contents so that you can find what you want relatively quickly. Check how accurate the table of contents is, and whether the page references, for example, do actually match the information in the contents list. Check too that the system used for page numbers does allow you to find the information you want quickly and easily. Some manuals will have systems that are easier for the reader, some that are easier for the writer of the manual! Most manuals will not be numbered straight through from page 1 to page 320, which is much easier for the reader, but will follow some other system, perhaps numbered within chapters or sections. The system that is used does not matter, as long as it is clear and the people who need to use the system can understand it. There are manuals which number only by sections, and pages can go by with no indication of where you are. Such manuals should be treated with a great deal of contempt.

There should be, then, an introduction or preface which tells you who the documentation is aimed at, what it will cover and what the person who has read it will know by the time it has been used. There should also be an accurate index, in every piece of documentation. Check the page references thoroughly. In addition, there should be effective cross-referencing, and pointers to where you should go for further information. A glossary is very helpful too, and is essential for first time users. Another point here is that different manufacturers and suppliers use different terms to refer to the same function. For example, some word processing systems will call a false left margin a "hanging indent", while others will call it a temporary left margin. If you don't know the precise term being employed, check how difficult the manual is to use. There are manuals available which provide a glossary of the terms used with the manual and which also contain the terms used by different manufacturers. This can be very useful.

Finally check the language used for consistency. If the manual interchanges words more or less at random while referring to the same activity, then it is going to be very confusing in practice. Using the word "file" consistently is going to be far more effective than using "file" and "document" as though they were synonyms. The problem here is that writers want to provide variety. Within a manual or piece of computer documentation, however, there is no room for such licence.

You will, I hope, have noticed that in this chapter, let alone book, we have used, for example, "documentation" and "manual" for substantially the same items. To say whether this is good or bad practice, you need to ask yourself who this book is for and what context it is written in. If it didn't confuse you at the time of initial reading, it may have achieved its purpose. If it did confuse you however...

The quality of the documentation supplied is therefore very important for the training manager. When your staff first start to use the system good documentation is essential. At the point where your staff has been trained to a reasonable standard, the quality of the documentation will make the difference between having an efficient system and one that does not function. Nevertheless, even good documentation is no substitute for proper training.

Now we will dispose of the blundering through type of training, where someone gleans information from whatever source is available and solves the immediate problem with it. In this method, both the person who organises the training, if that is an appropriate phrase, and the training itself, is a response either to a crisis or to an unexpected development. Since this whole chapter is devoted to avoiding this style of training, it will not form a major element in this discussion and we will dispose of it quickly here.

On the other hand, it is worthwhile recognising its existence, partly because as the person responsible for organising the training, you will want to be able to recognise those people who will not accept a training scheme and who insist on blundering through. As we have said, this could very well be your own manager, but it could be any member of the system staff. What you need to be clear about is how counter-productive blundering through can be. There are people who, for example, use accountancy software as a major element in their job. Because they have not been fully trained in using the application, much of the real work involved, such as calculating and recalculating specific functions which are already programmed in the application, is done, in the worst case, manually with a calculator and then the results are entered by hand or really equally pointlessly by writing complex formulae from scratch. To all intents and purposes, they are using the application program, and certainly getting results. In practice however, they are merely using the system as a sort of notepad or calculator. The good training manager will be aware of this possibility and take appropriate steps.

Blundering through can usually be recognised by the number of errors made both in using the terminal itself and in the results obtained. This should be another reminder that evaluation of the people who have been trained is a vital element in any training scheme. Everybody who has used computer systems at some stage will have blundered through a certain task, grabbing the minimum amount of information from whatever source, and then fudging the results. Often, the results will not be serious in themselves. Overall, they can be disastrous.

Having looked at documentation and a way of approaching training that cannot be recommended, we will look at the three types of training that you need to consider in detail. They should, however, not be seen in isolation, since they should complement each other. The strengths of on-line training, which we shall cover first, are only possible if backed up by proper off-line training, preferably with a formal element as well. Therefore, these three elements should be seen as part of the overall strategy, not for one to be chosen as *against* another approach. Indeed, the first one that we will cover, on-line training is not yet a suitable medium for a complete training course though the other two can be seen as working on their own where absolutely necessary. The particular strengths of on-line training do mean, however, that you should include some elements of it, if you possibly can.

On-line training, provided while a person is working on the system, can, then, be very valuable. With the minimum of preparation, a person can start to work with the system. Yet that minimum level of preparation is vital and needs careful planning. As yet there is no on-line training available which will allow a completely naive user to start work properly. The situation is changing rapidly in this direction, but we would view any claims in this area with scepticism until it is proved that this is no longer the case.

On-line training needs to be divided into three areas, but its major use must lie in the initial stages of learning a system, where a person is given directly the type of instruction necessary to start using the system. Thus, using an on-line system for reference about little used aspects of the system is technically possible now, but in practice would be so slow and irritating that it would be counter-productive. The sheer overhead on the system itself would be so large that it would probably degrade the system's performance to an unacceptable level for both the person seeking on-line reference and everybody else trying to work normally.

Thus, on-line reference materials should be regarded as unlikely to be much use. Under this heading **man**, or manual, the on-line reference supplied with many Unix type systems, will be seen as an encumbrance rather than a particularly useful utility. The real reason behind its existence may well be that it was a cheap way of distributing as much information as possible as quickly as possible. In that it succeeds, but it is not an effective training tool. For example, try the section on formatting a disk. It starts relatively easily, but soon becomes fairly hopelessly bogged down in minutiae, which really belong in a reference book which you can have open when puzzling through a problem. The quality of the reference materials in **man** usually leaves a great deal to be desired. As a rule of thumb, if you can understand what **man** is telling you, you probably didn't require any on-line reference material in the first place! It is noteworthy, too, that on many commercial systems **man** is too large an overhead for the system and is removed.

On-line guidance can be very useful however. If you know what a command is, but do not know exactly how to use it, it is very useful to have a method of receiving information about using the command, coupled with an actual example. This is for more advanced users.

The major use of on-line systems for training, however, lies in giving relatively naive users an introduction to actually using the system. Its advantage is that the new user can attempt to use the commands or functions and then be told where he or she went wrong. The interactive training this provides is a very effective and efficient method. What is more it is available whenever the person needs training, or even whenever the person has a gap in their own work-schedule. It can be quickly updated as the application or procedure changes. It is possible to make it an individual course, which keeps track of where the person was last time and also how well the trainee did. As a result, almost in private, a person can learn to use a procedure or function, try out using it and then, having simulated its use, really use it properly on the real system.

There are on-line training courses available. At the moment we do not feel that we can recommend them. They are either too much like a book, with simple screen flipping, or they are too tedious. The point here is to look out for any good materials that people do recommend. On-line training is developing very quickly, and as computer systems become more powerful, faster and capable of storing more information, they will inevitably make greater and more effective use of on-line training. On the other hand, you need to consider whether using a proprietary application program, like an authoring language or an authoring system, will allow you to create your own introductory materials which can be accessed while the system is in use. This sounds like a major investment, but it need not be, and it does mean that the expertise that is built up on running your system can be incorporated into your training and then distributed right across the system. As you will be able to check who has used the training, you will have a good idea of how effective this part of your training is.

Increasingly common now are cassette based training programs, mainly audio-cassette, but there are also some video-cassette programs. These do not really come under the heading of on-line training, but nor do they really come under self-study. Our view is that they have one major drawback at the moment: staff do not find them very motivating. Some are lavish productions, which spend a great deal of time introducing the course. Others are threadbare, and the courses themselves very sketchy. Our advice here is to be wary of such cassettes at the moment. They are fairly expensive, and of only limited utility.

One final point here is that many application programs are being supplied now with what is called on-line help. In most cases this is a very important part of the overall documentation. Check how good it is, by looking at the language used - how technical or how simple - and the ideas covered. Finally, you should also be aware of a refinement which is becoming far more common: context sensitive help. This means that the user does not have to choose the help that he or she requires, but the application supplies the right information at the right time. At the moment this is usually only a matter of assessing which command is being used at any particular time, but it is very useful indeed. It is well worth considering whether this is provided when working out which application packages to buy.

Perhaps the most common form of training supplied today is self- study materials. Indeed, many manuals, particularly in the micro computer world, come with a self-study section now. The advantages of such an approach is that in general such courses are cheap. They are available all the time and a person can take one home to study. They can be very effective and where they are not too odd in their choice of examples, they can motivate people to get to grips with an application package or system. The disadvantage is often contained in our last sentence. The examples are generally so much at a tangent to every day commercial life that they become too remote to be bothered with. For example, since many software companies are American, and West Coast American at that, the examples are drawn from American lifestyles which cannot pretend to be universal. One example that we know, created a scenario where the trainee had to manage an orange farm. On fine sunny days this seemed all right; on cold, damp winter afternoons it was very difficult to muster any enthusiasm for it. The most successful packages deal with something that a large cross-section of people do or have some contact with. If you want to produce your own self-study course but do not want to tie it to any particular department in your own firm, one good idea is to build a training course round a travel agency, since nearly everybody will have used one and have some interest in travel. If you want to assess how well people become motivated, you might try that idea.

The main drawback, however, with self-study materials is in the depth that they can treat their subject. Very often the limit is reached fairly quickly. There are very complex courses available, but they tend to be self-defeating. Knowing that a course will take a few hours a week for several weeks is one thing. Knowing that it is going to be like finishing "War and Peace" or a higher degree, is quite another. Some software and training companies have met this problem by adopting a two tier approach. The first offers an encouraging "Five minutes to . . .", followed by a more detailed course. This is worth thinking about. (Note, too, how this fits in with our view of how a course should be structured.)

The third type of training is the formal training usually found in a classroom, but which can be conducted in an office. In our view there is, at the moment, no substitute for it. On-line training and self-study materials either have their place or will have their place. Formal training needs these other elements too. Yet, formal training is where most really structured training will take place.

Its immediate disadvantage is that it is expensive. You have to pay for the trainer and the classroom, as well as the preparation and production of the course itself. In addition, you may have to pay travel and hotel costs of your staff. If the course is a general introduction, it may not fit your own specific approach and needs. On the other hand, if it is tailored to a particular application that you have on your system, the costs of producing it are likely to be excessive.

Nevertheless, there is no real substitute. It needs careful analysis, because its very cost means that it has to be effective. Yet that requirement for careful analysis is not a bad thing, as we hope this chapter shows.

Such formal training can take a variety of forms: in-house, using someone who has a flair for training; external, using a third party training institution, or even your system manufacturer or supplier.

There are two points that need to be stressed however. Even if the courses are external, do not rely on general - and they may well be called "intermediate" as I explained above - courses or introductions. Make sure that you know what the courses are aimed at and what the perceived point is. All reputable training establishments will have a document detailing their aims and objectives. Assess these carefully. Make a point of talking to the people who will be doing the training, not just to the sales people! After all, in computing as in other areas, people who are very expert at using systems may not be the best people to train others. Think back to school days, and remember whether music teachers, for example, were the best people to teach music to unmusical people. (In our experience they were the worst, since music was such an intuitive part of their lives, they could not understand how anyone could find music difficult. The same could well go for computer specialists.) You will also need to work out whether tailoring courses to your own needs might be worthwhile, too.

In the same way, you might consider having one member of staff trained formally and hope that this person will train the rest. This has been known to work, where the person chosen has had the skills and ability to understand the initial training course, communicate its information effectively and be able to understand precisely the needs of those being trained. On the other hand, good trainers are becoming increasingly expensive to employ, for the very good reason that they are scarce and also have very valuable skills. It might be possible to train just one person formally in a third party training establishment. The odds are relatively against this approach. Only you will be able to assess whether you are in fact setting up your own in-house training establishment, to match your training program, and whether this is either or both cost-effective and successful. As you can probably tell, our advice is not to follow this road, if all things are equal. Since they generally add up to a different number, you may have an answer in this approach.

Secondly, assess formal training in its own terms. The very word *training* is seen nowadays as quite a good concept. It has thrown off connotations such as education. It has, in the process, however, almost reduced itself to carrying out a series of activities like a squad being drilled. It is true that there are situations when using a computer which require absolute exactness and precision and a robot could do the job. In that case, try to find a robot, or at least use a batch file to do the work. Ninety per cent of the time, however, you want your staff trained to think things out for themselves, and for them to go beyond pressing control-d in an emergency. This brings us back to the concept basis for this approach to training. Skills have to be taught and learnt. What should also be acquired is an understanding of the reasons why things are as they are. In this sense, training here is much more than learning a drill.

Of course the training given depends on the person and the tasks to be undertaken. Yet nearly everyone will benefit from a view of formal training that goes beyond drills and simulations.

17.6 Who Needs to be Trained?

The simple answer to the question of who needs to be trained, is everyone who will be using the system. The better answer will examine the various groups of trainees, the types of tasks, the individuals concerned and the desired end result.

First of all you need to train yourself, on using the computer system, and then on using and managing your computer system. One way of assessing how good third party formal training establishments may well be using them yourself and assessing them against the points that you know to be valid for your own situation. Like all the training here, your own training is not a once and for all process: it is continuous. You will be learning every day, and you should use your log book to record what you have learnt, as well as considering whether you ought to turn that information into a course of some type.

Secondly you need to train a deputy: in case you are ill, on a course or just away on holiday. This is where it is important that you have a firm model of the system in your mind, and a firm grasp of the underlying concepts. As long as it does not conflict with the security of the system, you should be aware of the need for more than two people to have a good working knowledge of the system. Two people can be off work together, many times. But take the idea of deputies further: every time you think of a post that someone needs training for, make sure you also have at least one deputy for that position. It may be that you have many people entering data. Make sure, however, that the types of entry procedures are either identical or are familar to all, so that each can cover for everyone else.

Then you need to have a continuing program of training for your staff: recognising what they know already and then what they need to know, ending up with what it would be nice to know if there is time.

Record this information, as we suggested at the beginning. Secondly, recognise it. When someone has completed some training, on-line, self-study or formal, make a point of saying something or displaying the fact somewhere. Build in your rewards. You can say, for example: now that you understand this aspect, it is worthwhile training you to do this further and more difficult task. If you can, build in some tangible rewards too for people who achieve a good standard.

The final point is to see training not as an adjunct, a desirable extra, but as a vital part of the running of a computer system. Twenty years ago there was just about life in the idea that people had a job for forty years or so. Nowadays, a teenager can expect to be retrained something like once every ten years - at the outside. You will be changing your computer system at twice that frequency, probably once every five years. Training under such circumstances does not become an incidental, but an essential part of running the system.

Plan it carefully and know:

-What you want from training.

-What you want to train each person in.

-What sort of training you want to use.

-What type of approach to training you want.

-How to assess the training.

-That you must be prepared to alter your views as your understanding grows.

-Finally what priority you are giving to training.

Training, therefore, takes time, energy and resources. Not training people wastes time, energy and resources. That simple aphorism sums up the difference.

17.7 Checklist

Base training on reward and incentive.

Initially ask yourself:

-What do I want to achieve?

-What do I need to achieve?

-What are the requirements of my staff?

-What do I require of my staff?

3 levels of training:

-Introduction.

-Consolidation.

-Advanced.

4 parts to each level:

-Introduction of concept(s).

-Skills behind concept(s).

-Using skills.

-Evaluation of progress.

4 types of trainees:

    -Naive.

    -Basic knowledge.

    -Experienced.

    -People transferring from one system to another.

4 types of training:

    -Blundering through.

    -On-line training:
        -Tutorial.

        -Guidance.

        -Reference.

    -Self-study.

    -Formal training:
        -In-house.

        -External.

What to teach:

    -What people need to know.

    -What it is nice for people to know.

Documentation:

    -Physical quality.

    -Accuracy.

    -Appropriateness.

    -Table of contents.

-Page numbering system.

-Index.

-Glossary.

17.8 Conclusion

Training is expensive, but it is an essential element both of managing a computer system and managing people who work with computers. In the case of Unix and Unix-like systems, training is a fundamental requirement.

It is possible to create a training program by responding to immediate pressures and needs. The training course that you will produce will not be very strong or suitable. It will need constant changes and patches to allow it to meet changing demands.

If, however, you carefully analyse the approach you intend to take, your needs, the needs of your staff, the individual requirements of your system and the desired end result, you will have the basis of a durable, effective training program. Although this seems an elaborate and expensive way of proceeding, in practice it is far quicker and cheaper than the apparently simpler and cheaper alternative.

Chapter Eighteen

Planning to Survive.

System survival is what system management is all about. You must keep the system going. It must be able to survive the addition of new users, demands of new applications and the physical dangers which surround computer equipment. As part of your task of keeping the system up and running, you must plan for what might happen. Such planning can be divided into two parts: event planning and contingency planning.

18.1 Event Planning.

Event planning is easy to describe. It is the process of making decisions in the present, based on knowledge of what will happen in the future. This might seem to quite sensible, but it is often forgotten that seemingly unrelated matters may combine to affect what will happen, creating new and unforeseen events.

For example it is known that the expected life of a system is four years. Therefore when purchasing peripherals which will outlast the life span of the system, it is only wise to purchase items with a standard interface which, at least in theory, may be added to the replacement system.

As one gets closer and closer to an anticipated event, the need for planning what to do becomes more important. For instance, if your system supervisor is nearing retirement, you must think how newly recruited operators will fit into the structure.

This is fairly obvious but, in general terms, it is too easy to ignore future events. The answer is to keep an event book. As each future event is recognised in advance, it is written up and placed in the event book. These are usually loose leaf binders. When any decision is being made with respect to the system, you only have to look through the event book and evaluate how that decision will affect the events listed in the book. The opposite is also true, of course: how the events will affect the decision.

An illustration of this is the case of a finance house which was considering purchase of some extra terminals. Usage showed that they needed three extra terminals and competitive quotes were obtained from a number of suppliers. One of the suppliers made an offer to supply five terminals at a price only ten percent higher than the majority of suppliers were offering for three. It was, however, made clear that this offer only applied to purchases of a minimum of five at a time. If three were taken they would cost full price.

There was quite a bit of discussion about this within the department. The big problem was that if the funds were spent on the extra two terminals, money would not be available for the purchase of an additional printer/plotter.

When the event book was consulted it was noted that four terminals on the system would be past the age, three years, set by the service contractor as that which would be acceptable for service support, within the next year. Two, in fact, would pass the three year mark within the next six months. This meant that funding would have to be made available to replace these terminals anyway. It therefore made sense to take advantage of the current offer and use the money saved on the purchase of the two replacement terminals in six months time to purchase the printer/plotter.

18.2 Contingency Planning.

Event planning is based on the concept of planning for what you know will happen. Contingency planning is based on planning for what might happen.

It is not possible to have one specific plan which will cover all systems. Each system is different and a different plan must be developed to cover each one.

There are basic elements which should, however, exist in any plan:

-Emergency procedures: how you should respond to major emergencies, such as fire and flood.

-Backup procedures: the provision of secondary facilities to continue data processing in the event of failure at the primary site.

-Recovery plans: to restore full data processing facilities as rapidly as possible.

The plan itself should be a written document, or more likely a set of written documents. They should be consistent, simple to read and should not presume any degree of special knowledge on the part of anybody who may have to carry them out. It is no use writing instructions which only make sense to yourself. If the computer installation goes up in smoke, you might be inside, going up with it.

There should be at least three copies of the contingency plan: one kept on site; one at a backup location; one in a deposit store.

A major mistake made by many system managers is that they have plans to cope with disasters when they happen, but they do not write them down. Contingency plans must be written down, otherwise they are next to useless.

18.2.1 Risk Cost Analysis.

The first element you need to establish is: what is the possible financial cost of any risk. This cost should be calculated on an annual basis.

The formula for calculating this 'risk cost' is :

Annual Loss Exposure = Cost of Incident * Annual Frequency

You will see this formula expressed in many text books on contingency planning as ' ALE = I * F '.

It is important to work out these costs in advance, as you must be sure that the amount you are spending on loss prevention is less than the risk exposure.

We can look here at a couple of examples:

It is calculated that data entry clerks make on average three errors a day in entering data. The errors that are made are detected by a check routine. It generally takes the clerks ten minutes to find and correct each error. The time costs for each clerk, that is wages, employment overheads and system time costs, work out at £6 per hour. Therefore the cost for ten minutes is £1. The cost of correcting the errors, averages out at £3 per clerk per day. As there are ten data entry clerks on the system the total cost for correcting data entry is £30 per day. Allowing two hundred and fifty working days per year, this comes to an annual cost of £7,500.

To use the formula the number of incidents is 3*10*250: which is 7500, and the cost per incident is £1.

ALE = 1 * 7500

therefore ALE = £7500

If the cost of cutting down the number of errors being made by the data entry clerks is therefore less than £7,500, it is worth considering.

Be careful with this type of analysis, however. A scheme which would reduce the number of data errors by 50 per cent but would cost £5000 a year to run would not be economic.

Now for a second example:

An uninterruptable power supply, which will maintain constant supply to the system for 48 hours will cost £5,000. The present system will only maintain the system for 2 hours which is enough time to finish the jobs in hand and close the system down. The chances of a power cut lasting more than 2 hours are once in every 2 years, therefore the annual incident risk is 0.5. The costs of such an incident to the company would be the cost of paying unproductive staff plus the cost of getting the data processing carried out at another site. It is estimated that the cost for a serious power down might amount to £2,000. The new power supply, if installed, would need annual maintenence costing £500 per year and the cost would have to be written off over 5 years. Therefore the annual cost of the new power supply would be £1,500.

To put these into the formula:

Cost per incident = 2000

Frequency of incident = .5

therefore ALE = 2000 * .5

therefore ALE = 1000

This means that the cost of £1,500 per year is more than the risk exposure of £1,000. It is not economic to install the new unit.

Not everything is as cut and dried as the above illustrations and it can be quite hard to quantify either costs or damages. However, these need not be exact. Generally estimates are quite acceptable. In fact they can even be better. If too much time is spent on exactly quantifying the cost of a risk, it may well be that the cost of carrying out that exercise might exceed the savings produced.

18.2.2 Risk Analysis.

You should carry out a full analysis of every aspect of your company's involvement with computers, including how dependent the company is on specific aspects of its computer operation.

The most important part of this analysis is to build up a full picture of the importance of data processing tasks. In any data processing installation there are some jobs which must be carried out if the company is to continue to trade. There are other jobs which may be delayed for days, weeks, or in some cases, years, without any major impact on the company.

You must establish exactly what the impact of a loss of any process would be to the company. You cannot presume, of course, that because a task is minor to you, it is minor to the company. In one company a job which came up each month for the data processing manager, was to make an analysis of the weekly job sheets of the employees. This job took about half an hour a month and was generally fobbed off onto the most junior data entry clerk on the site.

Following a fire at the site, processing was transfered to the company's second site some distance away, where all the important programs were duplicated. No provision had been made, however, for the monthly job sheet analysis. Only when the report did not arrive in the accounts department, where it was normally sent via the wages department after they received it from the data processing department, did the data processing department find out that this report was the basis on which all charges were made to customers. Without this report no customers could be charged. A major disruption in cash flow was therefore caused with most invoices being nearly six weeks delayed before going out. As a result the company got into serious financial difficulties and became a target for a takeover.

18.2.3 General Interruption Planning.

The first contingency for which you have to plan is the ordinary event which can take place nearly every day in a data processing department. For example: what should be done if a file is erased in error, or what action should be taken when you get a disk read error.

18.2.2.1 The red book concept.

Events like those outlined above happen every day. You should develop procedures to deal with each type of event and write down the procedures that you do develop. These should be kept in a loose leaf folder. By keeping them in such a folder you can easily amend and update them as new techniques or better procedures become available.

Make sure that the description of actions to be taken is complete. It is no use merely writing: obtain the back up copy. Full details should be given on how to find out which back up copy needs to be obtained, who has it, and most importantly what method to use to restore it.

It has become common practice to place this material in a loose leaf binder which has a very noticeable cover. Normally this is red and it has led to such books being called the red book. In actual fact, of course, it does not matter what sort of cover you use, so long as it is easibly noticeable. Red does seem to be a good choice though.

What is important, however, is keeping the book up to date. Make sure it has a full and extensive index so things can be found without too much difficulty. As the System Manager you should check this book at least once a month to make sure all the information in it is correct and, at the same time, refer to your superuser's log. Each time, ask yourself whether there is anything which has come up which needs to be included. In addition, if a particular type of error seems to be occurring a lot, ask yourself whether you need to document how to cope with it.

18.3.2.2 The disaster plan.

When things do go wrong you must know how to deal with events. It is no use expecting to be able to work things out at the time. When writing a disaster plan a number of things should be kept in mind:

-It should be concise and easy to read, giving precise instructions on what should be done in certain events.

-It should give full details of the system used for making backups and where such backups are stored. There should be sufficient information here so that in the event of the site being totally destroyed, an outsider could take the plan and update the offsite backups to a current level.

-Where reciprocal agreements have been made to provide backup processing facilities with other sites, copies of those agreements should be included in the plan.

-The plan should include a full, up to date list of the addresses and telephone numbers of members of staff.

-It should include clear instructions of who is to be responsible for implementing the plan in case of a disaster. This should include second and third level replacement.

There are many more things which you may want or need to include. It would be well worth your while reading one of the specialist works on the subject of contingency planning. The most important point is to make sure that the plan is kept up to date and that copies are available to those who are likely to need them.

INDEX

222